NATIONAL GEOGRAPHIC
KiDS

# GiRLS CAN!

## SMASH STEREOTYPES, DEFY EXPECTATIONS, AND MAKE HISTORY!

Marissa Sebastian
Tora Shae Pruden
Paige Towler

NATIONAL GEOGRAPHIC
WASHINGTON, D.C.

# CONTENTS

SERENA WILLIAMS

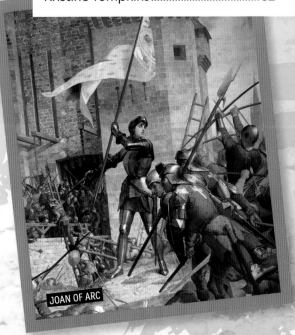

JOAN OF ARC

FRIDA KAHLO

SUSAN B. ANTHONY

VALENTINA TERESHKOVA

QUEEN ELIZABETH I DEFIED THE ODDS TO BECOME ONE OF ENGLAND'S GREATEST LEADERS.

CHAPTER **ONE**

# LEADER

SHIP

# GiRLS CAN... LEAD!

**CHANCES ARE YOU'VE HEARD OF QUEEN ELIZABETH, CLEOPATRA, AND JOAN OF ARC.** Incredible women like them have been ruling at ruling for centuries. Even so, an imbalance between the numbers of men and women in leadership positions has existed for millennia and still exists today. Some people even continue to believe debunked myths that women aren't natural leaders like men, despite plenty of evidence to the contrary. So what gives?

JOAN OF ARC

## THE RIGHT TO RULE

Women's access to the rights that were necessary for ruling—like inheriting and owning property, and having financial independence—have long been unequal to men's. Historians aren't sure how or why these inequalities in society first came about. One theory is that it all began when humans started to farm. Rather than continuing to share responsibilities, as many experts believe hunter-gatherers did, the men became farmers and warriors while the women stayed home to take care of the children. Over time, these gender roles led to the establishment of unequal laws for women. One such law was the practice of primogeniture, which meant that only a first-born son could inherit his family's estate. Primogeniture was practiced by most rulers around the world. Of course, some women still found ways to lead (as you'll see in this chapter). But only recently have some countries begun to get rid of these laws!

**MYTH #1:** WOMEN LACK AMBITION.

**FALSE!** In one study by leading management consulting firm McKinsey & Company, some 1,400 global executives, men and women, were surveyed and reported roughly equal desire to reach a top-level position. In fact, more women than men reported a strong desire to advance to the next level of their organization.

## WOMEN IN THE WORKFORCE

In Europe, women's rights worsened during the late Middle Ages with the creation of something called coverture. Coverture originally meant that a husband and wife shared their money. But it eventually came to mean that a wife was literally her husband's possession. In much of the Western world, a woman could not inherit or own property, maintain her own finances, or do much of anything without her husband's approval. Coverture made it incredibly difficult for women not only to rule but to enter the business world.

This imbalance lasted for centuries and still exists in some places. In fact, women in the United States did not join the workforce in large numbers until World War II (1939–1945), when they filled the jobs left vacant by men who were away at war. And even then, despite their growing numbers, working women faced discrimination. Many had to fight just to control their own finances, let alone be taken seriously for leadership positions. American women weren't allowed to apply independently for a credit card until 1974. Women have come a long way since then: The government estimates that women make up more than 45 percent of the American workforce. But only 4.8 percent of the top 500 American companies have female chief executive officers (CEOs).

**MYTH #2:** THE **WAGE GAP** EXISTS BECAUSE WOMEN DO WORSE AT THEIR JOBS.

**FALSE!** Long-term studies over 10 years show that even among women and men of equal skills, background, and training, women are often offered less advancement and have to deal with workplace bias and pay discrimination.

## STILL NOT EQUAL

In many parts of the world, women and men now have equal rights. Yet only 20.6 percent of the United States Congress is female. Studies also show that on average, American women only earn 53 to 85 percent of what men earn, with women of color facing the highest wage gaps. And despite the progression in women's rights, some people still claim that women aren't cut out for leading. But do these claims have any truth to them? Hardly! Take a look around this page to find out why.

## TIME TO LEAD

So, once and for all: Is it true that girls can't lead? No way! Not only does research back up the fact that women make excellent leaders, history does, too. In this chapter, you'll learn about women who became queens, empresses, prime ministers, CEOs, and more. Take a look at these powerful women who defied stereotypes, became respected leaders of their nations, and proved that girls can—and do—lead!

**MYTH #3:** WOMEN AREN'T BORN WITH THE SAME **LEADERSHIP SKILLS** AS MEN.

**FALSE!** There is no scientific evidence that men are born with a natural ability to lead, or that there is a large difference between the ways men and women lead. In fact, long-term studies showed that men and women ranked nearly equally as leaders in terms of skill and success. A survey conducted by *Harvard Business Review* found that female leaders ranked slightly ahead of their male counterparts and excelled in areas like initiative-taking and goal-making.

**ELLEN JOHNSON SIRLEAF** WAS THE FIRST ELECTED FEMALE HEAD OF STATE IN AFRICA AND THE FIRST BLACK FEMALE PRESIDENT IN THE ENTIRE WORLD. TAKE INSPIRATION FROM HER UNSTOPPABLE DETERMINATION!

Sirleaf **STUDIED ECONOMICS** at Harvard University.

# BECOME PRESI

WOMEN RALLYING FOR SIRLEAF DURING ELECTIONS IN LIBERIA

VOTE For Ellen PRESIDENT

## UNSTOPPABLE

Ellen Johnson Sirleaf was born in Monrovia, Liberia, on October 29, 1938. She was a good student and eventually left home to pursue her education in the United States. When she returned to Liberia in 1980, she began to serve her country as the minister of finance. Known for her honesty, Sirleaf often challenged the status quo. However, speaking against an established—and often corrupt—system also meant trouble. During national elections in 1985, Sirleaf criticized the reigning military regime, which had come to power through a violent overthrow. After speaking out, she was threatened with 10 years of imprisonment. Ultimately, Sirleaf avoided jail, but she was exiled for 12 years. This didn't stop her. Instead, she set her sights on a position that would allow her to speak her mind and make change.

## FROM EXILED TO ELECTED

During Sirleaf's exile, Liberia had again become a place of conflict. Since 1989, a warlord named Charles Taylor had been leading a rebellion known as the First Liberian Civil War. In 1997, Taylor overthrew the reigning military regime. That same year Sirleaf took the opportunity to head home and challenge Taylor for the position of president. She lost, however, and was quickly exiled again by Taylor. She wasn't allowed back into the country until 2003, when Taylor fell from power and was exiled from Liberia himself. Sirleaf still hadn't given up on her presidential plans, and in 2005, she ran for president again, promising to do her best to end conflict and corruption in Liberia. This time, she won. Sirleaf became Africa's first elected female president and the first black female president in the world.

Sirleaf and her administration got to work. Her goal was to create a united Liberia and help the country heal from its wars. Sirleaf was reelected in 2011 and continued to lead her country. That same year, she received the Nobel Peace Prize for her efforts. Some critics claim that Sirleaf did not accomplish all she set out to do, and that she often appointed her own family members to positions of power. However, Sirleaf's determination to lead her country into a peaceful era proved that women can overcome even the most challenging of obstacles. By refusing to be silenced, Sirleaf spoke for her entire country.

## LEAD LIKE SIRLEAF!

### BELIEVE IN YOURSELF

Sirleaf had confidence in her own ideas and opinions and knew that her thoughts were as important as anyone else's. Whether you're working on a group project, running for a leadership position, or looking for ways to improve your hometown—when you get a great idea, share it!

### BE PATIENT

It took Sirleaf decades to achieve her presidential goal, and longer than that to implement her plans for peace in her country. She failed more than once and faced difficult challenges. Be patient and remember that achieving a goal takes time and determination.

# DENT

U.S. PRESIDENT GEORGE W. BUSH PRESENTS SIRLEAF WITH THE PRESIDENTIAL MEDAL OF FREEDOM.

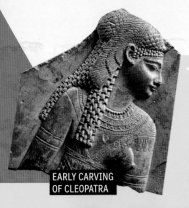

EARLY CARVING
OF CLEOPATRA

# MAKE HISTORY

**CLEOPATRA** WAS A SKILLED LEADER, A BRILLIANT TACTICIAN, AND A GIFTED SCHOLAR—ALL BY THE AGE OF 14. READ ON TO LEARN HOW CLEOPATRA USED HER LEADERSHIP AND WITS TO MAKE HISTORY—AND HOW YOU CAN, TOO!

**CLEOPATRA** is a Greek name and translates to "glory of her father."

## EARLY LIFE

In 69 B.C.E., Cleopatra VII Philopator (circa 69 B.C.E.–30 B.C.E.) was born into Egypt's Ptolemaic dynasty. She grew up learning advanced military strategies as well as eight different languages. When she was just 14, Cleopatra was made her father's heir alongside her younger brother, Ptolemy XIII. Cleopatra and Ptolemy XIII became co-rulers of Egypt when their father died four years later. However, ambitious Cleopatra had larger things in mind than ruling alongside her kid brother. Egypt had been an empire for thousands of years, but now its power was waning. Cleopatra believed it was up to her to return her country to greatness—so she seized control for herself. This upset many of Ptolemy's advisers. Alarmed by Cleopatra's independence, they exiled her into the harsh desert in 48 B.C.E. But Cleopatra did not give up easily.

## WITS AND WAR

Cleopatra was determined to reclaim her throne. Luckily for her, her exile coincided with unrest in the Roman Empire, another great power of the time. When the Roman leader Julius Caesar visited Egypt, Cleopatra saw her chance. Caesar was stationed at the palace in Alexandria. Perhaps if Cleopatra met with him, he would support her in the fight for control of Egypt. Plus, an alliance could also protect Egypt from Rome's ever expanding rule. But to meet with Caesar, Cleopatra first had to get back into Egypt and into the palace without being murdered by her brother's guards. As the story goes, she was smuggled into the palace in a rolled up carpet disguised as a gift for Caesar.

Her memorable entrance had its intended effect: Caesar restored Cleopatra to the Egyptian throne and drove her brother out of Egypt. Cleopatra and Caesar went on to have a child together named Caesarion, and through this powerful alliance, Cleopatra was able to keep Egypt independent. But despite her wit, Cleopatra's luck was poor; in 44 B.C.E., Caesar was assassinated, and Cleopatra found herself—and her kingdom—targeted once again.

## GOING DOWN IN HISTORY

After Caesar's assassination, while many political players scrambled to become Rome's new ruler, cunning Cleopatra quickly found another ally and love interest in Roman general Mark Antony. However, when Cleopatra and Mark Antony named Caesarion to be the true Roman heir, Caesar's nephew, Augustus, declared war. Augustus was victorious, and legend has it that Cleopatra and Mark Antony killed themselves rather than be captured.

After Cleopatra's death, Roman historians began to tarnish her reputation and put her down as a seductress who ensnared ill-fated men. This characterization lasted for thousands of years! Over the last century, however, scholars have uncovered the truth about Cleopatra's impressive rule. Though her enemies refused to believe it, Cleopatra actually succeeded at her ultimate goal: using her brilliance to secure a place for herself and for Egypt in history.

# LEAD LIKE CLEOPATRA!

### LISTEN TO EVERYONE

Unlike the previous Ptolemaic rulers, who preferred their native Greek, Cleopatra was the first Ptolemaic ruler to learn the Egyptian language of her people. If (and when!) you are in a leadership position, try to listen to those around you and be open to different points of view. You never know what great ideas you might get or new things you might learn!

### DON'T LET BULLIES GET IN YOUR WAY

Like many rulers, Cleopatra faced lots of criticism during her reign—and even for centuries after. But she knew exactly what she wanted and fought for it and didn't let other people, whether emperors or generals, intimidate her. People might disagree with you or your choices, but that doesn't necessarily mean you need to change course. Remember to stay true to yourself and focused on your goals. Your accomplishments will eventually speak for themselves!

ART DEPICTING CAESAR MEETING CLEOPATRA

# TAKE CHARGE!

**MARY BARRA** IS THE CHAIRWOMAN AND CEO OF GENERAL MOTORS COMPANY, AS WELL AS THE FIRST WOMAN TO BE CEO OF A WORLDWIDE AUTOMOBILE COMPANY.

Barra serves on the **BOARD OF DIRECTORS** of The Walt Disney Company.

## RACING TO THE TOP

Despite progress, women still face huge inequalities and obstacles in the world of business. The automobile industry, especially, has been historically unwelcoming to women. But Mary Barra was set on achieving in two worlds: business and cars.

Mary Teresa Makela was born on December 24, 1961, in Waterford, Michigan, U.S.A. Her father worked at the Pontiac car factory in Detroit, Michigan, and Barra was eager to follow the same path. After graduating from high school, she took a job inspecting car parts at General Motors to earn money for college. Her hard work paid off, and she received her degree in electrical engineering from the General Motors Institute in 1985. Barra stayed at the company and quickly moved up through its ranks. In January 2014, she became the first woman to serve as CEO of General Motors.

## TAKING THE WHEEL

Barra became CEO at a difficult time for the company. Its public image had suffered after some car models were revealed to have faulty parts. But Barra immediately issued safety recalls and took measures to create a safer company with better policies. She also drove the company toward technological advancements, including driverless cars, better safety equipment, and cars that produce fewer emissions. In 2017, General Motors created the world's first affordable electric car under her leadership.

While guiding her company into the future, Barra has also blazed a path for women in business; she currently ranks as one of *Forbes*'s most powerful women in the world. Under Barra's leadership, General Motors was recognized as one of just two companies in the Global Report on Gender Equality as having no gender pay gap. With Barra in the driver's seat, opportunities for women in business can only continue to grow.

# BE THE BOSS

## BOLD CHOICES

When Indra Nooyi (b. October 28, 1955) became CEO of PepsiCo in 2006, she joined an elite club. Only 10 women before her had been named CEO of one of the top 500 companies in the world. Born in India, Nooyi studied chemistry before she moved to the United States to continue her education at Yale University. She began her career at PepsiCo in 1994, as senior vice president of corporate strategy and development. Six years later, she became president and chief financial officer of the company, making bold decisions that would streamline the many food brands owned by PepsiCo. Her confident leadership made her a perfect candidate for CEO, and she stepped into the role ready to take PepsiCo—a company with an extensive history and long-standing presence across the world—to new heights.

## DESTROYING ANY DOUBT

At the time she became CEO, only 10 other women were leading companies of the same caliber, so Nooyi's performance was vital. They all had something to prove. But, as a woman of color, Nooyi faced even more doubts, as many questioned her capabilities because of her gender and race.

Nooyi never wavered: PepsiCo flourished under her leadership and doubled its overall revenue between 2006 and 2017. To make PepsiCo products healthier, Nooyi jump-started a plan to cut sugars, fats, and sodium from the company's products. She also focused on making sure the company was less dependent on sales of sugary soft drinks. Nooyi has been widely recognized for her impact on the company. She was included on *Forbes*'s Most Powerful Women list and topped *Fortune*'s Most Powerful Women in Business list in 2009 and 2010. In addition to serving as CEO, she was also the company's chairman of the board from 2017 to 2019. Nooyi's leadership not only ensured PepsiCo's success but also proved that women can take businesses to new heights.

Before she became a boss businesswoman, Nooyi **PLAYED GUITAR IN AN ALL-GIRL BAND.**

INDIAN-AMERICAN BUSINESSWOMAN **INDRA NOOYI** MADE HISTORY BY BECOMING A FEMALE *FORTUNE* 500 CEO. READ ON TO FIND OUT HOW YOU, TOO, CAN CRUSH ANY CAREER!

# SPEAK OUT

**VIOLETA BARRIOS DE CHAMORRO** WAS THE FIRST—AND TO DATE ONLY—WOMAN TO BE PRESIDENT OF NICARAGUA. FIND OUT WHY SHE IS CREDITED WITH BRINGING PEACE TO AN ENTIRE COUNTRY—AND HOW YOU, TOO, CAN MAKE YOUR VOICE HEARD.

Chamorro is known as **"DOÑA VIOLETA"** to friends and supporters.

## A PRESSING MATTER

Violeta Barrios de Chamorro (b. October 18, 1929) comes from a wealthy Nicaraguan family. The early years of her life were spent at private schools in the United States. When her father passed away in 1947, Chamorro returned to Nicaragua. There she met and married her husband, Pedro Joaquín Chamorro Cardenal. The marriage was important for Chamorro, not least because she began to help publish Cardenal's family's newspaper, *La Prensa*. The paper criticized the corruption in the Nicaraguan government. This led to Cardenal's murder. His death sparked the Nicaraguan Revolution led by a violent political organization known as the Sandinista National Liberation Front. Though she was in mourning, Chamorro refused to give up on *La Prensa*. She took over publishing the paper, unaware that she was setting the stage for her own presidency.

The Sandinista government swiftly began censoring newspapers in an effort to silence its enemies. Chamorro had once supported the Sandinistas, but she could not accept this censorship. Instead, she advocated for *La Prensa* to continue reporting on the government's treatment of its citizens. The Sandinistas took notice and threatened Chamorro with prison. They also banned *La Prensa* for a year. But she never backed down. In fact, this new regime and its policies ultimately became the reason Chamorro set her eyes on the presidency. Her tireless advocacy for freedom of speech eventually led to her nomination in the 1989 presidential elections. Chamorro ran on the promise to change major issues affecting the country, especially the ongoing civil war. But no one expected her to win. Chamorro was a political outsider with a complicated past, and, on top of that, she was a woman. No woman had ever been president. Yet Chamorro ran anyway—and won. After decades of dictatorship and 10 years of civil war, the future of the country was in the hands of Nicaragua's first female president.

CHAMORRO AND HER NEWSPAPER, *LA PRENSA*

## A LASTING LEGACY

Chamorro made good on her promise to end the war. She also reduced the government's military presence, reversed several Sandinista policies, and lifted censorship. Most important, she worked to unify a divided country. Though Chamorro retired after one term, the peace she worked so hard to achieve lasted for many years. Her belief in freedom of speech and in her own ability to lead helped forge a path for not only herself, but also for her country.

CHAMORRO DURING HER CAMPAIGN

## LEAD LIKE CHAMORRO!

### TRUST YOUR GUT

Chamorro believed in the importance of an uncensored press and freedom of speech, and she supported those rights in the face of intense pressure. She knew that it was necessary to speak out even though she would face criticism—and more. A good leader trusts their instincts and stands up for what they believe in—even when it's easier not to.

### USE YOUR SKILLS

Chamorro used her talent as a publisher to make her voice heard and give her leadership a platform. You, too, can use your unique skills—from painting posters to making new friends to creating fundraisers—to fight for what you believe in.

### CREATE UNITY

After a hard-fought election, Chamorro faced the task of unifying a divided country. Reaching out to opponents and working together to find solutions can help make people forget there was a conflict in the first place.

# GALLANT GALS

WHEN YOU THINK OF THE WORD **"HERO,"** WHAT IMAGES COME TO MIND?

**For many people, an imagined hero looks like a tall, brawny man with a sword and a shield.** Lots of stories show just this type of image again and again, leading people to associate heroes with physically strong men. As for women, many tales portray them as damsels in distress, waiting anxiously to be rescued by a hero. Others show them as princesses yearning for a valiant prince. Few depict women as the heroes. But throughout history, tons of real-life brave women have stepped up to save the day—and themselves—and managed to change history in the process. Meet some of the women who prove that girls can be heroes.

## JOAN OF ARC
### (circa 1412–1431)

Jeanne d'Arc (known in English as Joan of Arc) was born a peasant farm girl in northeastern France. Though Joan's life was simple, at the time France and England were embroiled in what later came to be known as the Hundred Years' War (circa 1337–1453). By the time Joan was 17, France seemed to be losing. But Joan felt a calling, claiming higher powers charged her to deliver France to victory, and she managed to convince the eldest French prince, Charles VII, to give her an army to take into battle. Not only did Joan lead her army into a tide-turning victory at the Battle of Orléans, she also helped install Charles as king. However, soon after, French politicians—frightened by her rising power—handed her over to the English, who tried her for heresy and burned her at the stake. Joan of Arc remains a French folk hero to this day.

## QUEEN NANNY
### (circa 1680s–1740s)

During the 17th century, millions of African people were captured and forcibly sent to the Americas for slave labor. One such person was Nanny, a woman stolen from her home in West Africa and sold into Jamaican slavery. But Nanny fled and joined the Maroons—enslaved people in the Americas who had escaped and formed their own communities. Nanny went on to found a safe haven called Nanny Town and became the leader of a group called the Windward Maroons. Queen Nanny, as she was known, formed a military resistance against the British slaveholders, leading attacks and freeing hundreds of enslaved people. By some accounts, she is credited with saving almost 1,000 people. Queen Nanny is beloved to this day and considered a national hero in Jamaica.

## QUEEN BOUDICCA
### (died circa 60 c.e.)

Boudicca was the queen of the Iceni tribe of northern Britain and was married to King Prasutagus. They had an uneasy truce with the Romans, who had invaded Britain some 20 years before. However, when King Prasutagus died, he made a fateful mistake: He left his fortune to the reigning Roman emperor. The move was likely an attempt to secure Roman protection for his family. Instead, the Romans annexed Prasutagus's land. But they weren't counting on Boudicca: The queen fought against the Romans by uniting Celtic tribes and revolting. She successfully led an army in driving the Romans out of multiple cities and outposts. Although Boudicca was eventually overthrown by Roman governor Paulinus, she stands to this day as a British national heroine.

## RANI VELU NACHIYAR (1730–1796)

As a young princess in Tamil Nadu, South India, Velu Nachiyar developed ferocious skills; it was said that she could both fight and shoot arrows from horseback. Nachiyar married the king of Sivagangai and gave birth to a daughter and became Rani (queen) Velu Nachiyar. When British forces invaded the kingdom and killed her husband, she was forced to flee. But Nachiyar's fighting skills served her well: She built powerful resistance armies (including an all-female army), blew up multiple British ammunition stockpiles, and successfully recaptured her kingdom and installed her daughter on the throne. Nachiyar became the first Tamil woman to revolt against the British colonization of India.

# INTERVIEW WITH
# NANCY PELOSI

Nancy Pelosi is an American politician who has served 17 terms as a congresswoman. In 2007, Pelosi made history by becoming the first woman to serve as speaker of the United States House of Representatives. Reelected to the role in 2019, Pelosi leads the section of Congress known as the House of Representatives and is second in the line of presidential succession after the vice president.

## WHAT DO YOU THINK IS THE MOST IMPORTANT CHALLENGE FACING WOMEN TODAY?

 **PELOSI:** I think a barrier for many women is a question of confidence. I just say to them: Know your power, be yourself, there's nobody like you.

## WHAT DO YOU THINK IS THE MOST IMPORTANT CHANGE THAT NEEDS TO HAPPEN FOR WOMEN IN THE NEXT 10 YEARS?

 **PELOSI:** If I ruled the world, I would say—and this is in keeping with National Geographic—the education of women and girls throughout the world is the most significant transformation that we can make. It's important for women individually, for their families, for their economies in their countries, for the societies in which they live.

## WHAT IS YOUR MOST CONSPICUOUS CHARACTER TRAIT?

 **PELOSI:** Strong. Sometimes people say I'm tough, and I'm thinking: It's not tough; I'm strong. I think I have strength. And the strength sprang from my purpose, my knowledge, my strategic thinking. I'm not going to fold from weakness. I may concede on the strength of your argument, but I'm not folding from weakness.

## WHAT WOULD YOU SAY IS YOUR GREATEST STRENGTH?

 **PELOSI:** My confidence. And giving people the credit they deserve and then some. Women have to have each other's backs. Because there are those who still feel threatened about the world changing in a way that they're not ready for.

## WHAT'S YOUR ADVICE TO YOUNG WOMEN?

 **PELOSI:** My advice to young women: Know your purpose, know your why, know your what, know your subject, show your plan, connect, listen to people, connect to people. With that, you will be a leader.

# CHRISTIANE AMANPOUR

After fleeing Iran at 11 years old during the 1979 Iranian revolution, Christiane Amanpour became deeply passionate about investigating and covering global stories of conflicts and the people affected. She went on to become one of the leading journalists for CNN, ABC, and PBS. In addition to shedding light on historic national events, Amanpour has received multiple awards, including numerous Emmys for her dedication to bringing global attention to areas of conflict.

## WHAT DO YOU THINK IS THE MOST IMPORTANT CHALLENGE FACING WOMEN TODAY?

**AMANPOUR:** The most important challenge is still being considered second-class citizens, despite the progress. Despite 100 years since some women got the right to vote, despite all the personal achievements of women in just about every field you can name, there is still an institutional prejudice against women. An institutional bias. The most important thing for us is to get men on our side, period. It is not a question of just swapping who's dominant. We're not looking for female dominance; we're looking for equality and to level the playing field—and we can't do that without men's buy-in as well.

## WHAT DO YOU THINK IS THE SINGLE MOST IMPORTANT CHANGE THAT NEEDS TO HAPPEN FOR WOMEN IN THE NEXT 10 YEARS?

**AMANPOUR:** Women need to get equal pay for equal play. And women need to do what they started to do, and that is turn out in droves for elections—not just to vote, but to stand for office. This will be game-changing for women because many, many, many, many do their utmost and break barriers from the sidelines—but unless it's institutionalized, and until it's institutionalized, it won't have that tipping-point effect.

## WHAT ADVICE WOULD YOU GIVE TO YOUNG WOMEN TODAY?

**AMANPOUR:** I would tell young women that there's nothing that they cannot do, but they mustn't expect things to be given to them. They mustn't have any sense of entitlement; they must simply be prepared to do the hard work, as I would say to any boy as well. Then, not only do you deserve what you achieve, but you become an expert, you become confident—because you've accomplished and mastered all the steps between starting out and getting to a position of influence and success. I think that's really, really important. And to young girls I would simply say what probably women have told them from time immemorial: Never take no for an answer.

SHE WASN'T EVEN SUPPOSED TO BE QUEEN. BUT **ELIZABETH I** OF TUDOR ENGLAND WOULD TURN OUT TO BE ONE OF THE GREATEST RULERS OF ALL TIME!

Elizabeth I was known for her **LOVE OF HORSEBACK RIDING.**

# DEFY
# EXPEC

## UNDERESTIMATED FROM DAY ONE

Born in England in 1533, Elizabeth I (September 7, 1533–March 24, 1603) did not grow up in line for the throne. The fact that she was a girl disappointed her father, King Henry VIII. Soon after, he had Elizabeth's mother beheaded so he could marry a third wife, Jane Seymour. The king's government then declared that only Seymour's children could ascend to the throne, making Elizabeth's path to ruling even more unlikely. After her father's death in 1547 and her half brother's soon after, there were no eligible male heirs left to rule England. But even then, Elizabeth wasn't the first female choice! She didn't take the throne until yet another death occurred: that of her half sister, Queen Mary.

As queen, Elizabeth led a country that was in ruins. It was weak and recovering from years of war. There was little money, and threats of new wars pressed in from surrounding countries. Even some of the queen's own advisers tried to undermine her. But Elizabeth quickly set up a group of trusted advisers and a spy network throughout England. She focused on developing natural resources, expanding trade, and encouraging the arts. Her policies were effective, and she quickly won over both her court and her people.

## INDEPENDENT WOMAN

As England grew in size and wealth, so did the flood of suitors eager for the queen's hand in marriage. Yet she refused to marry, which helped maintain a delicate balance between the superpower countries for many years.

Despite Elizabeth's fierce attempts to avoid war, tensions grew too great. In 1588, the king of Spain declared war and sent the powerful Spanish Armada, a fleet of more than one hundred warships, to conquer England. The smaller English navy was thought to be no match for the Spanish Armada. But Elizabeth refused to give up. She journeyed to the coast of the battleground and rallied her troops in person. Encouraged, the British set upon the Spanish with vigor. With better tactics and some luck, the English triumphed and sent the Spanish Armada home.

After defeating the Spanish, Elizabeth used the great victory to guide her country into a new era of peace, wealth, and growth. What became known as the Elizabethan age—under the reign of a queen who was never supposed to rule at all—England entered one of its greatest literary periods, emerged as a world leader, and enjoyed 44 years of success and prosperity.

## LEAD LIKE ELIZABETH!

### EXPECT THE UNEXPECTED

Elizabeth had no way of knowing the role she'd play in England's history—it wasn't supposed to turn out the way it did. But when the opportunity arose, Elizabeth relied on her determination, education, and trusted advisers to turn an unexpected situation into success.

### LEAD BY EXAMPLE

During her rule, Queen Elizabeth faced attacks and intimidation from those tasked with "advising" her. Rather than submit to their attempts to subdue or bully her, she fought back by being the best leader she could be, even forming her own vast spy network and delivering stirring speeches to her troops. Remember that you can't always win over everyone you meet, but you can set a good example by acting with poise and grace in the face of conflict.

ART SHOWING QUEEN ELIZABETH I RALLYING HER TROOPS BEFORE A BATTLE WITH THE SPANISH

# TATIONS

# RISE TO
# POWER

## AN UNLIKELY RISE

Wu Zetian (circa 624–705 C.E.) was born Wu Zhao under the Tang dynasty (618–907 C.E.). At age 14, she began working at the royal palace as a low-ranking maid. But crafty Wu found her way to the side of Emperor Taizong and became his companion. After Taizong's death, it was expected that Wu would be sent to a Buddhist convent. Instead, she caught the eye of his son, the new emperor Gaozong, and they had a daughter together. With this stroke of luck, Wu quickly found a way to eliminate her female rivals and rise in the court's ranks, though historians disagree about the exact methods. Wu's critics claimed that she murdered her own daughter (the baby is known to have died in infancy) and framed Gaozong's wife, the empress, for the death. Others believe the story is simply slander created by Wu's many political rivals. Though history may not know her exact methods, Wu went on to establish herself as Gaozong's wife and empress consort and ensured her future by having rivals executed or exiled from China. When Gaozong died, Wu declared herself the ruling empress.

AS CHINA'S FIRST FEMALE RULER, **EMPRESS WU ZETIAN** WAS ACCUSED OF BRUTAL CRIMES. BUT SHE WAS ALSO BELOVED BY MANY FOR HER EFFECTIVE POLICIES.

Wu created her own set of Chinese characters known as the **ZETIAN CHARACTERS.**

## EVIL QUEEN OR GREAT RULER?

Wu's rise to the throne was not without opposition. It was unheard of for a woman to rule, and several officials and politicians revolted. But no revolt succeeded because the people of China loved Wu. She was a capable leader, and China prospered under her rule. Some of her most popular policies included the expansion of Chinese borders and reopening the Silk Road trade route. Her improvements extended to the daily lives of common people as well. She lowered taxes, funded new public works, established public education, and shared information about improved farming techniques. Despite these achievements, Wu has largely been remembered as a villain. Although Wu likely did engage in treacherous—and deadly—politics, her rivals just as likely exaggerated or invented her crimes. For the historians of her time, Wu's greatest crime was daring to rule China as a woman, and that was inexcusable to them. Wu's lasting achievement as an empress stands, however. She created a unified and flourishing country during her rule.

# BUILD EMPIRES

## THE PATH TO POWER

Around 240 C.E., Julia Aurelia Zenobia, also known as Septimia Zenobia, was born in Palmyra, the capital of a Roman province covering the territory of modern-day Syria. Zenobia's early life was most likely peaceful and pleasant. Though the Roman Empire had conquered Palmyra in 64 C.E., the province remained fairly independent. Zenobia had been born to a wealthy family and grew up riding horses and learning Greek, Latin, Egyptian, and Aramaic. She eventually became the wife of Palmyra's Roman-appointed governor, Odaenathus.

Elsewhere in the Roman Empire, things were not as tranquil. Rome was engaged in a war against the Persians and facing multiple rebellions in the north of the empire. Zenobia's husband, Odaenathus, was able to repel approaching Persian armies, saving Palmyra and the province. As a reward, he was named governor of the entire Roman East. However, he and his eldest son were soon assassinated, leaving his younger son Vaballathus to rule. But Vaballathus was too young, so Zenobia named herself regent.

## ESTABLISHING AN EMPIRE

Unlike her husband, Zenobia was not content to remain under Roman rule. She immediately took control of the eastern territories that the Persian army had lost, and then seized areas that now make up all of Syria and large parts of Turkey. In 269 C.E., she captured Alexandria, the capital of Egypt. By the following year, she controlled all of Egypt and had declared the Palmyrene Empire's independence.

Zenobia now ruled an empire nearly equal in size to Rome. She was said to be an imposing force, and the emperor of Rome, Claudius Gothicus, recognized the Palmyrene Empire. But in 270 C.E., Emperor Gothicus mysteriously died, and Lucius Domitius Aurelianus rose to the position. Unlike Gothicus, Aurelianus refused to accept the Palmyrene Empire's independence—especially when ruled by a woman. Aurelianus marched against the Palmyrene Empire with his entire army. Zenobia and her son were taken prisoner, and the Palmyrenes surrendered. Though sources tell conflicting stories about Zenobia's defeat and eventual death, her cunning, defiance, and brilliance became legendary.

**JULIA AURELIA ZENOBIA** NOT ONLY CHALLENGED THE ROMAN EMPIRE—SHE ESTABLISHED AN EMPIRE OF HER OWN!

Russian empress Catherine the Great supposedly often compared herself to **ZENOBIA.**

## YAA ASANTEWAA
LED THE ASHANTI PEOPLE IN A FIGHT FOR INDEPENDENCE FROM BRITISH RULE, PAVING THE WAY FOR GHANAIAN INDEPENDENCE.

AN ARTISTIC RENDERING OF ASANTEWAA

**ASANTEWAA** was the only woman in the history of the Ashanti Empire to be named war leader.

THE QUEEN MOTHER'S STOOL. THE ASHANTI BELIEVE THAT A PERSON'S STOOL HOLDS HIS OR HER SOUL.

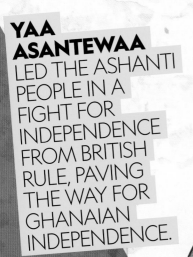

# LEAD

## A QUEEN MOTHER'S REBELLION

In the Ashanti Empire, women had access to power and leadership positions. The kingdom, which lasted from 1670 to 1957 in what is modern-day Ghana, awarded women seats on village councils and included them in important decision-making. Yaa Asantewaa (circa 1840–October 17, 1921) was to become one of the most powerful Ashanti women of all. Born to humble beginnings, Asantewaa made a living as a farmer. But when her brother, chief of the Ejisu people within the Ashanti Empire, was exiled, her life changed quickly. Her brother named Asantewaa queen mother of the Ejisu in his absence. Asantewaa ruled peacefully, but she soon faced a new challenge.

In the early 1800s, the Ashanti had begun trading items like gold and ivory with the British. But by the end of the century, the relationship between the two empires soured. The British seized Ashanti land, arrested its king, and exiled all of its rulers. Soon, the British demanded the Golden Stool, the most sacred symbol of the Ashanti nation. The Golden Stool, which was said to contain the soul of the Ashanti people, symbolized the rights of its possessor to rule. Should the stool fall into British hands, it would not only mean

humiliation—it could mean defeat. Asantewaa refused to give up. To encourage her fellow leaders, she said, "If you, the men of [Ashanti], will not go forward, then we will. I shall call upon my fellow women ... We will fight till the last of us falls on the battlefield." From then on, Asantewaa was viewed as more than the queen mother; she was now the war leader of an Ashanti fighting force of 5,000.

## FROM EXILE TO FREEDOM

In March 1900, Asantewaa and her troops laid siege to British forces. After the British sent more than 1,000 expertly armed units, Asantewaa and her closest advisers were captured and exiled. By January 1902, the Ashanti Empire officially became a British territory. Asantewaa died in exile in 1921. Just three years after her death, the Ashanti rulers and leaders were allowed to return home. Asantewaa's remains also made the journey back to the Ashanti Empire for a proper burial. Eventually, in 1957, Asantewaa's dream came true when the Ashanti Empire found freedom as part of the nation of Ghana. Asantewaa's brave resistance inspired those who came after her to fight on for their freedom.

# LEAD LIKE ASANTEWAA!

### PLAY THE LONG GAME

Asantewaa didn't get to see her dream of independence realized, but she held fast to her hopes and fought for it anyway. Success usually doesn't happen overnight. Be prepared to work hard—and for a while—for the things that are important to you.

### ENCOURAGE OTHERS

When most had given up, Asantewaa inspired those around her to take a stand. Remember that the more people you can inspire to join your cause, the more likely it is to succeed.

### AND RELY ON THEM, TOO

Being a good leader also means trusting those who are helping you with your cause. Asantewaa's fight for independence continued after she was gone because others carried on her dream.

ART DEPICTING THE BRITISH TAKING OVER THE ASHANTI EMPIRE

# ARMIES

# MELINDA GATES

In 2000, Melinda Gates co-founded the Bill and Melinda Gates Foundation—the world's largest private philanthropic organization—alongside her husband, Bill Gates. The foundation aims to reduce inequality around the world by providing access to health care and education, combating disease, and promoting women's empowerment. To date, the foundation has an endowment of around $50 billion. In 2016, Gates and her husband were awarded the Presidential Medal of Freedom by President Barack Obama.

## WHAT IS YOUR GREATEST STRENGTH?

**GATES:** I draw a lot of strength from family—and from my kids in particular. I've known almost my whole life that I wanted to be a mother, and when I had my children, they changed everything for me. I stayed home with them when they were young, but they're also the reason I decided to take on a more public role at our foundation. I wanted them to see me out there in the world living my values and doing everything I could to put my beliefs about equality and social justice into action. I love them first and foremost for who they are but also for who they make me want to be.

## WHAT ARE THE BIGGEST HURDLES YOU HAD TO OVERCOME?

**GATES:** I went to an all-girls school where we were told every day that girls could do anything. But, like a lot of women, when I got into the workforce, I realized the rest of the world hadn't quite caught up to that message. When I started at Microsoft, I was often the only woman in the room, and that can have an effect on you. These days, I spend a lot of time thinking about the biases and barriers women encounter in the workplace. From a policy perspective, I think there's a lot more we could be doing to make sure that women are equally empowered to succeed at work—paid family and medical leave, for one.

## WHAT DO YOU THINK IS THE SINGLE MOST IMPORTANT CHANGE THAT NEEDS TO HAPPEN FOR WOMEN IN THE NEXT 10 YEARS?

**GATES:** You could answer this question a lot of different ways, but there is strong evidence that helping women exercise their economic power is one of the most promising [ways to reach] gender equality. When women have the chance to earn an income and exercise decision-making power over the money they make, it changes everything for them and for their families. One study found that when mothers in Brazil had control over their family's money, their children were 20 percent more likely to survive—that's an astonishing statistic.

# ELLEN PAO

American businesswoman Ellen Pao is an activist and CEO who promotes diversity and inclusion in the technological world. Previously, Pao spent almost a decade facing gender discrimination and bias as a woman working for a tech investment firm. In 2012, she filed a gender discrimination suit against her employer, but went on to face online harassment and discrimination while working as CEO of a social media site. Pao used these experiences to found a nonprofit—of which she is CEO—that works with tech start-ups to foster inclusion and diversity.

## WHAT DO YOU THINK IS THE MOST IMPORTANT CHALLENGE FACING WOMEN TODAY?

 **PAO:** The hardest challenge is getting fair treatment and being treated equally, based on ability to contribute, based on skills. That makes it hard for women in the workplace, and in society, to figure out how they need to behave because they're often not treated fairly when they behave in a natural way that's comfortable to them.

## WHAT DO YOU THINK IS THE SINGLE MOST IMPORTANT CHANGE THAT NEEDS TO HAPPEN FOR WOMEN IN THE NEXT 10 YEARS?

 **PAO:** We need to see more women in leadership positions, and specifically more women of color, in order to make sure that people are actually treating women fairly and creating fair workplaces. It takes women and women of color at the highest level.

## WHAT ADVICE WOULD YOU GIVE TO YOUNG WOMEN TODAY?

 **PAO:** It's really important to know what you want and then to find a path to get what you want—and not to be driven by what other people want for you or what opportunities seem available for you. Doors are opening and there are more opportunities, but they're not universal—so you do need to do some work to find them. You need to find situations where there is somebody who's willing to help you, show you the ropes.

## WHAT DO YOU THINK IS YOUR MOST CONSPICUOUS CHARACTER TRAIT?

 **PAO:** I try to be an advocate. Speaking up for others, especially people who aren't able to, is really important to me.

Born in a time and place where women were granted fewer rights than men, Benazir Bhutto (June 21, 1953–December 27, 2007) flipped the script by taking charge of not only her own life, but also the Pakistani government. Bhutto's early life was unusual for a woman in mid-20th-century Pakistan. Her wealthy family was deeply involved in politics: Her father, Zulfikar Ali Bhutto, founded a major political party in Pakistan called the Pakistan People's Party (PPP) and eventually was elected prime minister. The PPP sought to ensure that all Pakistani citizens had their needs met. Bhutto's father encouraged Bhutto to get an education, which wasn't common for Pakistani women at the time. Bhutto excelled at her studies and attended Harvard University at only 16 years old. Later she studied political science, philosophy, and economics at the University of Oxford. She returned to her home country, but two years later political unrest led to her father's death and the repeated arrest and imprisonment of Bhutto and her mother. Faced with no other options, she left Pakistan for London in 1984.

Bhutto's childhood nickname was **PINKIE.**

**BENAZIR BHUTTO** MADE HISTORY AS THE FIRST WOMAN TO HEAD A DEMOCRATIC GOVERNMENT IN A MUSLIM NATION AND SERVED AS PRIME MINISTER OF PAKISTAN FOR TWO SEPARATE TERMS.

# WIN ELEC

BHUTTO SPEAKING OUT AFTER HER IMPRISONMENT IN PAKISTAN

PAKISTAN PEOPLE'S PARTY POSTER

## TAKING CHARGE

Having maintained her connections with her father's political party, Bhutto returned to Pakistan in 1987. She married and became pregnant while still vocally opposing Pakistan's president. Proving that pregnancy and motherhood are not obstacles to leading, Bhutto campaigned hard for the PPP, and the party won the next election in May 1988. Bhutto had become prime minister of Pakistan. Despite objections from some who believed a woman could not lead the country, her first term lasted until 1990, and Bhutto was elected prime minister again in 1993. She became a founding member of the Council of Women World Leaders, an organization created specifically for female heads of state across the world.

## ENDLESS INSPIRATION

Despite her wins, Bhutto faced continued criticism. She became unpopular with other Pakistani politicians and was accused of corruption and had to leave her country once again. She fought hard to disprove the charges and was granted amnesty and allowed to return home after eight years. Celebrations of her return were cut short when she was tragically killed while campaigning for an upcoming election.

Bhutto is celebrated worldwide for changing the perception of women in government in the Middle East. Her persistence in the face of obstacles and threats has inspired countless women to control their own narratives.

## LEAD LIKE BHUTTO!

### BE BRAVE

Bhutto grew up in the middle of political unrest and was exiled at a young age. But she knew that fighting for your dreams—whether it's getting an education or becoming the first female prime minister of a Muslim country—matters, and she battled on. It can be scary to put yourself in the spotlight or face people who disagree with you, but it is worth it to make a difference.

### STUDY HARD

When Bhutto ran for prime minister, many people believed that women should not—or could not—lead. But Bhutto was an expert politician and had studied for many years, and she easily proved them wrong. With lots of skill and knowledge under your belt, you can change even the most stubborn of minds.

# TIONS

Tompkins was named a **UN ENVIRONMENT PATRON OF PROTECTED AREAS** in 2018.

A DEDICATED CONSERVATIONIST WHO ALSO HAPPENED TO BECOME A HIGH-IMPACT CEO? **KRISTINE TOMPKINS** IS ONE EXCELLENT EXAMPLE OF HOW TO TURN YOUR PASSION INTO A POWERFUL PROFESSION.

## PATH TO PATAGONIA

Kristine Tompkins (b. June 30, 1950) has always loved the outdoors, and she spent much of her childhood climbing, hiking, and exploring. When she turned 15, she landed a part-time job at rock-climbing legend Yvon Chouinard's budding climbing equipment business. In 1973, she and Chouinard expanded the business into Patagonia, Inc., selling clothing and gear for multiple outdoor activities. The name came from the region in southern South America that is known as one of the last places in the world where untouched nature still exists. But like many regions across the planet, the amazing natural resources of Patagonia have been under threat from practices such as logging and deforestation.

# BLAZE TRAILS

## CHIEF *ENVIRONMENTAL* OFFICER

Tompkins eventually became CEO of Patagonia, Inc., and focused on creating a business that would actually benefit the world.

In the 1980s, the company began donating portions of its profits to environmental organizations. Tompkins also helped form One Percent for the Planet, a program that has companies donate either 1 percent of sales or 10 percent of profits—whichever is larger—to environmental causes. Patagonia, Inc., also committed to making its stores energy friendly and sustainably sourcing materials for its products. By the time Tompkins's retired as CEO in 1993, her impact as a leader and environmentalist was immeasurable—and she was just getting started.

## FROM ONE PATAGONIA TO THE NEXT

After Tompkins left Patagonia, Inc., she and her husband moved to the region Patagonia. Together they created two organizations, Tompkins Conservation and Conservación Patagónica, which allowed them to focus on preserving nature on a global scale. Over 22 years, they are credited with preserving more than 14 million acres (5.6 million ha) and donating more than $300 million. In 2018, Tompkins helped announce the establishment of two new national parks in Chile. Her goal is to create at least five more parks in Patagonia. Tompkins continues leading the charge to save our planet, one acre at a time.

## WHAT DO YOU CONSIDER TO BE YOUR GREATEST STRENGTH?

**TOMPKINS:** Certainly perseverance, as well as loyalty—whether it's loyalty to national parks or loyalty to friends and family—and determination. The things I've done in my life tend to be starting something, or being part of something, that's new and usually difficult; those are the kinds of environments I seem to like.

## WHAT DO YOU THINK IS THE SINGLE MOST IMPORTANT CHANGE THAT NEEDS TO HAPPEN FOR WOMEN IN THE NEXT 10 YEARS?

**TOMPKINS:** There will be no healthy women on a dead planet. So to have true rights and equality for women, there has to be [a healthy environment] for all humans. That's the broad picture.

## WHAT WOULD YOU SAY IS THE BIGGEST CHALLENGE THAT WOMEN FACE TODAY?

**TOMPKINS:** Self-confidence.

## WHAT ADVICE WOULD YOU GIVE TO YOUNG WOMEN TODAY?

**TOMPKINS:** I would say that you need to go for things, trust your instincts, and remember that luck is often a product of hard work. And don't worry about what people are going to think about you. Don't worry about failing or succeeding, just go for things because you think they're the right thing.

TOMPKINS SPEAKING UP FOR THE ENVIRONMENT

CHAPTER **TWO**

# SPORTS
# &ADVEN

# TURE

# GiRLS CAN ...
# PLAY SPORTS!

HOW OFTEN HAVE YOU HEARD THE PHRASES "THROW LIKE A GIRL" OR "RUN LIKE A GIRL" USED AS INSULTS? Throughout history, many people have believed that women couldn't play sports or engage in physical activities. Some people also believed that women shouldn't do these things, even if they could. But why?

## PLAY LIKE A GIRL

Probably the biggest obstacle facing women who want to play sports is the false idea that sports aren't appropriate for them. For thousands of years and across many cultures, society has dictated that certain activities are appropriate for men, while others are appropriate for women. Anything considered "manly," such as physical activities, was viewed as improper for women. This even led to women being banned from some sports entirely! Women were forbidden from competing in the Olympics (which began in 776 B.C.E.) until the 1900 Paris games. Even then, the inclusion of women caused a scandal because many people, both men *and* women, still saw women's participation in sports as immodest, unladylike, and a danger to traditional social roles. Even after women were allowed to compete in the Olympics, their choice of sport was limited.

It wasn't until the Summer Olympics in London in 2012—when women were finally allowed to compete in Olympic boxing—that women achieved equality to men in Olympic events. But it wasn't just the Olympics.

Women were also barred from the Boston Marathon until 1972, and many women's teams and leagues weren't founded until recently—the U.S. women's national soccer team was formed in the 1980s, for example, even though men had been competing in the World Cup since the 1930s.

Today, women have more opportunities to compete than ever before, but the playing field still isn't equal. Many sports, such as football, don't have professional women's leagues in the United States despite an abundance of female athletes. On top of that, professional female athletes are paid much less than their male counterparts and still contend with biases and outdated stereotypes. Do any of the myths on this page about women in sports have any truth to them? Read on to find out!

## WINNING LIKE A GIRL

Despite strong interest and ability, women still face many hurdles in the sports world, from combating stereotypes to a lack of opportunities. But many female athletes are pushing the boundaries, from baseball to tennis to aviation. Get ready to meet the ladies proving that girls can not only play sports, but also win.

### MYTH #1: SPORTS ARE **TOO DANGEROUS** FOR WOMEN.

**FALSE!** Believe it or not, many people used to believe that physical activities were dangerous for women. Gender stereotypes around the world held that women were delicate and physically unable to stand much exercise. Some doctors—from ancient times right up through the early 1900s—even claimed that too much exertion would make it impossible for women to have children or would damage their internal organs. Modern science easily disproves these false notions. Researchers have found that when women train in the same programs as men, they experience the same overall benefits and increases in health.

**FALSE!** Some people label sports with lots of physical contact as "boy sports," while those with less physical contact are called "girl sports." But these categorizations are just a continuation of gender stereotypes that have stuck around through history. They've been around for so long that athletes are still more likely to choose sports within their stereotypical roles. But these gender roles are made up: Just as many boys and men excel at dance, volleyball, and figure skating, and many girls and women are fantastic hockey players, boxers, and wrestlers.

### MYTH #2: THERE ARE **DIFFERENT TYPES OF SPORTS** FOR GIRLS AND BOYS.

### MYTH #3: WOMEN'S SPORTS **AREN'T AS POPULAR** BECAUSE PROFESSIONAL FEMALE ATHLETES **AREN'T AS SKILLED AS MEN.**

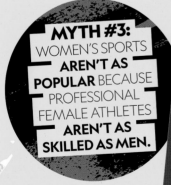

**FALSE!** The lack of women's sports on television and in the media isn't a measure of the worth or talent of female athletes. It's actually another form of gender stereotyping. Sports media often do not cover men's and women's sports equally, which influences viewers' perceptions. Men's professional sports dominate television, creating big branding opportunities for companies and celebrity male athletes. One study showed that women's sports receive just 4 percent of all sports media coverage. On top of that, another study found that even when the media do cover female athletes, reporters are three times less likely to focus on sports and athletics than when covering men. Instead, the focus is often on appearances, age, or personal relationships.

# BE THE BEST

## SERENA WILLIAMS

CURRENTLY HOLDS THE RECORD FOR THE MOST GRAND SLAM SINGLES TITLES OF ANY ACTIVE TENNIS PLAYER, MALE OR FEMALE, AND IS REGARDED AS ONE OF THE GREATEST ATHLETES OF ALL TIME.

## A SERVE AWAY FROM STARDOM

Serena Williams (b. September 26, 1981) seemed destined for the court. Born in Saginaw, Michigan, U.S.A., Williams had a tennis racket in her hand by age three. Her parents, Oracene Price and Richard Williams, who coached both Williams and her sister Venus—also a top player— played a vital role in Williams's journey to becoming a record-setting athlete. Under their guidance, Williams made her professional tennis debut in 1995 at 14 years old, just a year after her sister. In 1999, Williams won the U.S. Open tennis championship, earning her first great victory and first Grand Slam title. It seemed that nothing could stop her.

## AN UPHILL BATTLE

Although Williams continued collecting win after win, some of her greatest battles came off the court. She faced discrimination from a young age, encountering racism within the tennis world. Her father has often described what it felt like to hear parents of white junior tennis players talking about his young daughters in offensive ways. Even after Williams's professional debut, open discrimination from tennis fans, critics, bystanders, and even officials continued. Despite Williams's incredible skill and talent, many media organizations focused on her appearance, scrutinizing her hair, outfits, and physical looks. Others criticized Williams's strength, claiming that she appeared "too masculine." But none of this stopped her.

SERENA AND VENUS WILLIAMS TOGETHER

Williams reached the finals of **TWO GRAND SLAM TOURNAMENTS** less than a year after giving birth to her daughter.

## ALWAYS A WINNER

Williams refused to be intimidated. Despite the discrimination, she went on to win 22 more individual Grand Slam titles, as well as four Olympic gold medals. She's also won 14 doubles titles with Venus and holds the most individual tournament victories among both men and women. And her achievements don't stop on the court. Williams has had success in the world of business, creating a line of clothing inspired by her own bold style.

Williams has fought discrimination head-on. In an open letter in 2016 and a later essay in *Harper's Bazaar* magazine, Williams called out double standards she faces, such as unequal treatment from umpires. She also made note of the fact that some people still refuse to acknowledge the heights of her skill, calling her "one of the world's greatest female athletes" rather than "one of the world's greatest athletes," as she has proven herself to be.

With a career now spanning three decades, Williams continues playing championship-level tennis. When she added another title to her long list of achievements—Mom—it became yet one more way she is leading and inspiring women everywhere to push the boundaries of what it means to be an athlete—male or female.

## TRIUMPH LIKE WILLIAMS!

### BE FOCUSED AND FIERCE

Williams became a champion at a young age, and she hasn't stopped winning since. She is fiercely dedicated and has never let critics and naysayers stop her from achieving her goals. Find what you love and practice as much as you can!

### GET IN THE GAME!

Williams is an exceptionally gifted athlete, but you don't have to be the best to take on the challenge of trying a new sport or activity. Try your hand at different sports and activities, give it your all, and take a chance!

WILLIAMS PLAYING AT THE 2016 U.S. OPEN

# FLY HIGH!

## KATHERINE SUI FUN CHEUNG
WAS THE FIRST CHINESE WOMAN TO OBTAIN HER INTERNATIONAL FLYING LICENSE.

Founded in 1929, the **NINETY-NINES INTERNATIONAL ORGANIZATION OF WOMEN PILOTS** still exists today.

## AIMING FOR THE SKY

At 17, when Katherine Sui Fun Cheung (December 12, 1904–September 2, 2003) moved to the United States, she had no idea that her destiny would eventually take her to the skies. When it was time for her to learn to drive a car, Cheung's father brought her to Dycer Airport in Los Angeles, California, to practice. That was when she first laid eyes on airplanes and fell in love with aviation. But when she asked her parents for flying lessons, she was met with a resounding no.

By 1931, Cheung, married and a mother of two at that point, hadn't given up on her dreams of flight. In fact, she had managed to convince her family that she should take flight lessons and planned to move back to China and enroll in flight school. But Cheung met with disappointment again. The aviation school in Guangzhou (formerly known as Canton) did not permit women to enroll. Yet Cheung was not dissuaded. She stayed in the United States and began training with the Chinese Aeronautical Association at Dycer Airport, where she had originally fallen in love with airplanes. Under the tutelage of the experienced pilot Bert Ekstein, Cheung's dream finally began to take off.

## ACHIEVING GREAT HEIGHTS

In 1932, Cheung not only became the first Chinese woman to earn a flight license, she also began flying as a daredevil stunt pilot. Cheung flew upside down and in spiraling dives; she performed barrel rolls and dizzying loops. Her skills led to her performing in stunt shows all along the California coast. Cheung's popularity soared, and in 1936 she was invited to join the Ninety-Nines—a famous all-female aviation club started by Amelia Earhart, the first woman to fly solo across the Atlantic Ocean. Cheung also went on to become the first Chinese woman licensed for commercial air travel. Though Cheung had dreams of returning to China to open a flight school, she decided to retire from flying after her father passed away. In just one decade, she had made her mark on the aviation world and inspired countless women everywhere by defying many gender stereotypes and societal expectations. Cheung demonstrated that women belong in the cockpit as much as men. For her, it just made sense. As Cheung said, "I wanted to fly, so that's what I did."

# BREAK **BARRIERS**

## BORN DETERMINED

Bessie Coleman (January 26, 1892–April 30, 1926) was born in Atlanta, Texas, U.S.A. Coleman's family lived in poverty: Her father was a share-cropper, and her mother was a maid. Much of Coleman's early life was spent in cotton fields or in a small school for black children. Coleman, who was half black and half Native American, often faced intense racial discrimination. By the time she was 18, Coleman had diligently saved enough money that she earned by picking cotton and washing laundry to enroll in college.

## NO MORE "CAN'T"

Unfortunately, Coleman's money didn't last long, and soon she had to leave school to get a job. She moved to Chicago, Illinois, U.S.A, to live with one of her brothers and find work. Coleman's brother told tales of serving in France during World War I (1914–1918). At the time, French women were allowed to work as pilots, but American women were not. So her brother teased her about yet another thing that she could not do: fly. But Coleman was done with being told that she *couldn't*. She became determined to earn her wings. She packed up her things, used what money she had, and moved to France in November 1920. By June 15, 1921, she was flying.

## A HIGH-FLYING LEGACY

After getting her pilot's license, Coleman received advanced flight train-ing to become a stunt pilot. When she finally returned to the United States, "Queen Bess" dominated the exhibition flight circuit. For five years, cheering crowds watched as she took to the skies and completed stunts no one else even dared to try. Having achieved one dream, Coleman decided to use her popularity to make another dream come true: She would open a flight school to train black pilots. Unfortunately, a tragic accident during preparation for an air show resulted in Coleman's untimely death on April 30, 1926. But she had made her mark. Today, many people credit Coleman with breaking down barriers, not just for black female pilots but for all women in aviation.

**BESSIE COLEMAN** OVERCAME POVERTY, RACISM, AND SEXISM TO BECOME THE FIRST BLACK WOMAN AND THE FIRST NATIVE AMERICAN WOMAN TO EARN A PILOT'S LICENSE.

Coleman took **LANGUAGE CLASSES** to apply to flight schools in France because the application had to be written in French!

# DIG DEEP

IN 2013, NATIONAL GEOGRAPHIC EMERGING EXPLORER **MARINA ELLIOTT** LED A TEAM OF CAVERS DEEP UNDERGROUND TO RECOVER AN IMPORTANT DISCOVERY: THE REMAINS OF A PREVIOUSLY UNKNOWN HUMAN RELATIVE.

## THE CALL TO ACTION

Imagine a new action-adventure film, in which a daring team of scientists descends into a deep, dark cave to uncover Earth's mysteries. For Marina Elliott (b. August 5, 1969), this movie-worthy scenario became reality. Elliott, who grew up in Calgary, Canada, had spent time working as an archaeologist in Siberia and Alaska, U.S.A., hoping to discover important fossils belonging to ancient humans and their relatives. In 2013, Elliott learned that National Geographic Explorer Lee Berger was assembling a group of scientists to recover fossils from a cave in South Africa. And he was looking for a very specific group of daring scientists—people small enough to fit into the narrow chutes and deep recesses of the Rising Star cave system. They would have to descend 100 feet (30.5 m) and squeeze through narrow, 8-inch (20.3-cm) openings in near darkness. Elliott applied immediately.

## IN THE DARK

Elliott joined the team, known as the "underground astronauts," in November 2013 for the Rising Star expedition. Their goal was to find a way through the twisting paths of South Africa's Rising Star cave system and uncover a trove of fossils. Two cavers had accidentally discovered the fossilized bones, but it was up to the archaeologists to retrieve them.

As the senior caver on the team, Elliott was the first inside. The group had to cross a dark, narrow passage called "Superman's Crawl" on their bellies. Then they had to clamber through an area called "Dragon's Back" before finally descending a vertical 39.4-foot (12-m) chute. Elliott successfully navigated each challenge, arriving at the discovery of a lifetime. The team found bones that belonged to a never before discovered member of the great

Homo naledi would have lived around 236,000 TO 335,000 YEARS AGO.

ELLIOTT IN THE RISING STAR CAVE

ape family known as hominids! The discovery proved there is another part of the human family tree that scientists had never known about before. Working in groups of three for six hours at a time, the team spent more than three weeks recovering all 1,500 bones. The haul was the largest of its kind ever made in Africa.

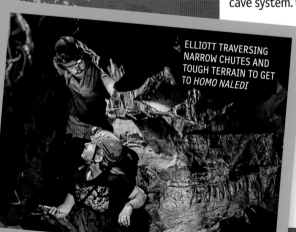

ELLIOTT TRAVERSING NARROW CHUTES AND TOUGH TERRAIN TO GET TO HOMO NALEDI

## EXPLORING THE FUTURE

Named *Homo naledi* by scientists, the recovered fossils are a vital scientific link to the origin of humanity. Elliott's contributions to the scientific community—both physical and archaeological—are immeasurable. She is excited to continue exploring the Rising Star cave system. When asked about her hopes for the future, Elliott said, "It's just exciting to realize that the great age of exploration isn't over with, that there are places to explore and there are things to find. That's pretty cool."

## TRIUMPH LIKE ELLIOTT!

### GIVE IT A GO

Elliott had the opportunity to be part of a history-making expedition because she sought it out. She wouldn't have been invited to join the team if she hadn't applied. Elliott went for it, and so should you!

### NEW OPPORTUNITIES

Think it's all been done before? No way! Elliott couldn't have known the fossils she helped recover would lead to such important groundbreaking discoveries. But they did! Remember that there are always new inventions, ideas, and discoveries to be made.

### UNEARTH YOUR TALENTS

Elliott's background in archaeology and experience with caving made her the perfect choice for the Rising Star expedition. Take pride in your unique talents and the activities you love, and learn new skills whenever you can— you never know how you'll be able to apply them.

# BROADER BEAUTY

## IS **BEAUTY** REALLY IMPORTANT?

**Despite the fact that women have made incredible athletic, scientific, historic, and cultural contributions to the world (as you've seen in this book!), they still struggle with something known as the "feminine beauty ideal"—it** refers to the idea there is somehow only one definition of beauty that applies to everyone. Society and the media still place enormous value on a woman's physical appearance, and companies make millions by promoting the false idea that a woman needs to look a certain way to be considered beautiful. Historically there's been big money in preying on a person's insecurities, from skin lighteners and tanning creams, to weight-loss teas and photo-editing software. But women are pushing back! Meet five women who are destroying old-fashioned beauty standards and celebrating their self-worth.

### JILLIAN MERCADO

Jillian Mercado is a Dominican-American disability rights advocate. She is also a model who has spastic muscular dystrophy. Mercado has committed herself to raising awareness for the one billion people in the world who encounter discrimination as a result of their disabilities. She has appeared in campaigns for House of Deréon—Beyoncé's former clothing line—Galore, Diesel, *Glamour* magazine, and more. In 2018, she visited the United Nations to discuss efforts to address the inequality facing people with disabilities. Jillian says that "having a disability doesn't stop [her] from doing anything. It's an honor and a privilege to show people that it's okay to be yourself and still do what you love."

## ERNESTINE SHEPHERD

Ernestine Shepherd can bench-press 115 pounds (52 kg). And she's more than 80 years old! Although her strength may fly in the face of many stereotypes about age and gender, that wasn't Shepherd's original goal. When she turned 56, Shepherd and her sister made a pact to get fit, aiming to become the world's oldest bodybuilding sisters. Unfortunately, Shepherd's sister, Velvet, soon fell ill. Before she passed away, Velvet made Shepherd promise that she would continue their mission and inspire other senior citizens to get healthy. Shepherd took the promise to heart: She holds the world record for oldest performing female bodybuilder, runs marathons, enters competitions, models, and inspires people around the world.

## GEENA ROCERO

Born in Manila, Philippines, Geena Rocero moved to New York City to pursue her dream of modeling. She became a successful transgender model and was featured in prestigious campaigns and on runways. But Rocero wanted more. Having faced discrimination in her own life, she was determined to advocate for equal rights for others in need. In addition to modeling, she now works as a producer and gives inspirational talks that promote understanding, recognition, and equality for transgender people. Rocero also founded Gender Proud, a global organization that works to advocate for and represent the transgender community.

## JAMEELA JAMIL

Jameela Jamil refuses to be defined by the numbers on a scale. An actress and a model, Jamil grew tired of having her appearance and body commented on in the tabloids, and of seeing young girls on social media worry about their weight. So she began I Weigh, a campaign that encourages people to redefine weight as more than just a number, focusing instead on their unique traits, such as kindness, intelligence, curiosity, and more. The campaign quickly went viral, inspiring a growing movement against diet companies and airbrushing.

## MADELINE STUART

Madeline Stuart wanted to be a model. She also happened to have Down syndrome, a genetic disorder that can cause intellectual disabilities and developmental differences. The modeling world is not always known for being inclusive, and for many this dream wouldn't have come true. But not for Stuart: She refused to give up and became the world's first professional model with Down syndrome. She has appeared in world-famous shows at New York Fashion Week and Paris Fashion Week, and she has modeled for famous publications such as *Vogue*. Stuart also advocates for diversity and inclusivity.

THE **ALL-AMERICAN GIRLS PROFESSIONAL BASEBALL LEAGUE** (AAGPBL) WAS A WOMEN'S LEAGUE MADE UP OF 10 TEAMS. IN ITS ERA, THE LEAGUE GAVE MORE THAN 600 WOMEN THE OPPORTUNITY TO PLAY PROFESSIONAL BASEBALL, AND TODAY ITS LEGACY CONTINUES TO INSPIRE ATHLETES.

The popular movie *A League of Their Own* was inspired by a real AAGPBL team, the **ROCKFORD PEACHES.**

# CHANGE THE

THE ROCKFORD PEACHES, MEMBERS OF THE AAGPBL

## PLAY BALL!

The United States' entry into World War II impacted countless industries. But more than manufacturing and production jobs were at stake. With fewer men available to play and fewer people to attend games, American Major League Baseball was in peril. Philip K. Wrigley, chewing gum mogul and owner of the Chicago Cubs Major League Baseball franchise, assembled a committee to tackle this problem. Their solution: an all-female softball league. It was a shocking idea because, at the time, women weren't taken seriously as athletes. But with financial backing from other team owners, the committee got to work. Women's softball already existed, so to make this new game more interesting, they established rules that more closely resembled baseball's. With the rules of the game in place, their next step was to find players for their league.

## LADIES OF THE LEAGUE

The women who took those first spots in the AAGPBL were scouted from softball teams across the United States and Canada. The first women signed were Claire Schillace, Ann Harnett, Edythe Perlick, and Shirley Jameson. Overall, 60 women took part in the first season.

Unlike the contracts presented to the men of Major League Baseball,

MEMBERS OF THE FORT WAYNE DAISIES

the women of the AAGPBL had to sign contracts that included strict rules about their appearance and behavior. They were expected to avoid short hairstyles, required to wear lipstick in public, and never permitted to smoke or drink in public. And to make sure they were "ladylike," the women had to attend etiquette and hygiene classes. Even their uniforms were designed to be "feminine": The women had to play in short skirts, even though they were sliding and running. Punishment for breaking the rules was harsh: When left fielder Josephine "JoJo" D'Angelo got a haircut that was deemed "too short," she was cut from her team. But not even sexist rules and uniforms stopped these athletes from playing ball.

Early on, many who came to watch the games viewed the league as a joke—how could women possibly play baseball? But once they saw the players' skills, they changed their minds. Slowly, public perception turned around and fans came in droves as the league expanded. By 1948, the league attracted an impressive 910,000 fans.

PLAYERS OF THE MUSKEGON LASSIES OF MICHIGAN AT SPRING TRAINING

## LASTING LEGACY

Although the war ended in 1945, the women's league continued for almost a decade after that. By the time the AAGPBL closed in 1954, the 600 athletes who played in the league had made their mark. To this day, their jerseys and memorabilia are displayed in the National Baseball Hall of Fame. After the league closed, many women played wherever they could, often in recreational softball leagues. But the AAGPBL remains legendary, and its influence is still felt today: In recent years, women's Little League Baseball has made a comeback.

# GAME

# SHATTER
# RECORDS

### FACING HURDLES

Tegla Loroupe (b. May 9, 1973) was born in Kutomwony, Kenya, and discovered her love of running when she was just seven years old. Unfortunately, Loroupe's father declared that being a runner was too unladylike and tried to ban her from the sport. Even Athletics Kenya (which governs sports in Kenya) deemed Loroupe too frail to be a runner. But she never gave up, and the federation was forced to reconsider its decision after Loroupe won a prestigious cross-country race when she was just 15.

### ON THE RIGHT TRACK

Now impressed by Loroupe's abilities, the federation nominated her for the 1989 Junior World Championships. She finished 28th on her first attempt. But five years later, in 1994, she ran her first major marathon in New York City and won! The victory made her the first African woman to win the New York City Marathon. (She even went on to win the race a second time.) Her win also marked the first time Kenya had a female runner who ranked alongside its male athletes. Loroupe continued to have success, setting new records. She went on to break the world marathon record, and, to date, Loroupe still holds world records for the 20-, 25-, and 30-kilometer distances. She is also a three-time IAAF World Half Marathon champion.

### RUN FOR PEACE

After gaining international attention for her achievements, Loroupe was determined to use her fame as a platform for world change. In 2003, she founded the Tegla Loroupe Peace Foundation, a charitable organization that aims to promote peace through sports. A few years later, in 2006, Loroupe launched the 10K Tegla Loroupe Peace Race, successfully bringing together 2,000 warriors from six different warring tribes. Loroupe is also an active member of Champions for Peace, a group of athletes that aims to bring about peace and harmony through the camaraderie of sports. In addition to her extensive philanthropic work, Loroupe continues to inspire women across the globe who are told that they can't participate in sports.

**TEGLA LOROUPE** IS A RECORD-BREAKING LONG-DISTANCE TRACK AND ROAD RUNNER WHO USES SPORTS TO PROMOTE PEACE.

Loroupe's childhood nickname was "CHAMETIA," which means "the one who never gets annoyed."

# CONQUER CHALLENGES

### THE EARLY RACES

Mokgadi Caster Semenya (b. January 7, 1991) was born in Limpopo, South Africa. She discovered that she loved running races at just six years old. As a junior athlete, Semenya broke an impressive number of records. When she competed in the 2009 African Junior Championships, she won the 1,500-meter race with a time of 4:08.01, and the 800-meter race with a time of 1:56.72, breaking the junior *and* senior South African records for both distances. Semenya seemed poised to take on the track world.

### A CAREER CHALLENGED

Semenya competed in her first race at the 2009 World Championships in Berlin, Germany, and dashed to victory in the 800 meter with a time of 1:55:45, more than two full seconds faster than any of her competitors. It was an amazing win. In fact, her performance was so remarkable that critics began to question Semenya's ability—and even her body. People claimed that she was too muscular and too fast to be a woman. Eventually, the International Association of Athletics Federations (IAAF) required Semenya to submit to gender tests. She endured almost a year of testing and calculations and was not allowed to compete until the IAAF reached a conclusion. While awaiting the decision, Semenya also faced ruthless public scrutiny and was mocked by the media.

### A BITTERSWEET VICTORY

In July 2010, an IAAF panel confirmed that Semenya's World Championship victories were valid. But the results of her gender verification tests, which were supposed to be confidential, were also leaked, revealing intimate details about her anatomy and that she did in fact have higher than typical natural testosterone levels. She endured even more public abuse when this news came out. The IAAF has since proposed new regulations targeting female-identifying intersex athletes specifically, which is a hurdle Semenya will continue to face. But one thing is clear: Her extraordinary resilience in the face of so much opposition continues to be an incredible inspiration to people everywhere.

**CASTER SEMENYA** IS A SOUTH AFRICAN RUNNER WHO SHREDDED RECORDS. BUT SHE ALSO FACED EXTREME SCRUTINY BECAUSE SHE WAS SO FAST ON THE TRACK.

Nike sponsors Semenya and has featured her in one of its **SHOE CAMPAIGNS.**

# RIDICULOUS MYTHS & LAWS

## ARE **SPORTS** BAD FOR WOMEN?

Over the years, people have believed some pretty bizarre—and now fully debunked—things when it comes to women participating in sports. At various times, it's been thought that women were too delicate to participate in physical activities. Or that it was improper and unladylike for women to sweat, compete, or wear "masculine" athletic attire (whatever than means!). These outdated and incorrect ideas led to some wacky myths and controlling laws concerning women. Check out some of the weirder ones.

### BICYCLE FACE

When the bicycle became popular in Europe and the United States in the late 1800s, women began to ride in droves. But many male doctors, who may have been alarmed by the newfound freedom women were experiencing on their bikes, cautioned that riding bicycles could cause insomnia, depression, and heart troubles in women. They also said it could lead to "bicycle face," a permanent change in a woman's face caused by the strain of bicycling. Of course, none of this was true, and the myth of bicycle face had pretty much disappeared by the 20th century.

## BUSTED FOR BATHING SUITS

Though women today compete in many kinds of swimming competitions, women in the past had a difficult time just finding practical bathing suits to wear. In the late 19th century in the United States, women wore heavy flannel dresses and bloomers to go in the water. As swimming became a more common pastime and women began to partake in water sports, their suits slowly became more practical. But they were regulated by law. Officers patrolled beaches and were responsible for measuring the lengths of women's swimsuits. Any woman whose suit was deemed too "revealing" could be arrested.

## WATCHING THE OLYMPICS

For a long time, women were not allowed to compete in the modern Olympics. But during the Olympics in ancient Greece, which lasted from 776 B.C.E. to 393 C.E., most women weren't even allowed to watch. Although unmarried women could attend the games (and even sometimes compete in separate footraces), married women were banned entirely and could be punished by death for breaking the law.

## ORGANS ON THE MOVE

The ancient Greeks believed that a woman's internal organs could randomly move around her body and result in many serious health issues. (Spoiler alert: The internal organs in your body—whether you're male or female—cannot simply wander around to other areas.) This myth persisted through the early 1900s, and one German doctor even theorized that running could damage women's internal organs.

# CLIMB TO

TABEI OVERCAME INCREDIBLE ODDS TO BECOME THE FIRST WOMAN TO SUMMIT EVEREST!

## CLIMBING LADIES

During the late 1960s and early 1970s in Japan, women didn't typically take part in extreme sports or adventures such as mountaineering. But Junko Tabei (September 22, 1939–October 20, 2016) had fallen in love with mountain climbing at just 10 years old after a class trip to climb Mount Asahi and Mount Chausu in Japan. Tabei continued to climb as an adult but kept encountering strict cultural expectations. "Back in 1970s Japan," she said, "it was still widely considered that men were the ones to work outside and women would stay at home." This made it difficult for Tabei to find climbing opportunities and to challenge herself. Many men refused to be her climbing partner, and some even accused her of climbing just to meet men! But Tabei decided to keep at it—for herself and for no one else. In 1969, Tabei formed the Ladies Climbing Club: Japan. Over the next three years, with the help of her climbing club, Tabei summited Mount Fuji in Japan and the Matterhorn in the Swiss Alps. But the ultimate climbing challenge still loomed: Mount Everest.

## TAKING ON EVEREST

When she decided to climb Everest, Tabei did so with a group of 14 other women who called themselves the Japanese Women's Everest Expedition (JWEE). Made up of teachers, computer programmers, and mothers, JWEE worked hard to gather supplies and trained extensively to prepare for their expedition. In early 1975, they set out. The first part of the trek went smoothly; the group had almost reached their goal when a major disaster struck. Early in the morning on May 4, a massive roar from the mountain signaled an avalanche. A sea of rushing white overtook their camp, burying the group alive. In an interview from 2016, Tabei recalled being pinned underneath her four tentmates before blacking out. The team's guides yanked Tabei out of the snow by her ankles. Miraculously, every member of the climbing group survived. Bruised but determined, Tabei continued her climb. Twelve days later, she made history: Navigating a steep mountain edge and crawling on her hands and knees, Tabei became the 36th person—and the first woman—to successfully climb Mount Everest.

# THE TOP

The highest point in the world, **MOUNT EVEREST** reaches 29,035 feet (8,850 m).

## TRIUMPH LIKE TABEI!

### PUSH YOURSELF

Tabei was hooked on mountain climbing from her first experience and always sought to improve and challenge herself while climbing. She pushed herself to her limits, and so can you. Set challenges and goals for yourself, and then try to beat them.

### FIND STRENGTH IN FRIENDSHIP

When Tabei couldn't find a supportive team or climbing partner to help her improve, she reached out to others and created her own group. Not only did she get the help she needed, but she inspired others at the same time. Don't be afraid to ask others for help—and to give help when others need it!

## REACHING THE TOP

Tabei had triumphed over Everest, but she didn't stop there. In her lifetime, she completed more than 69 major climbs. In 1992, she successfully climbed the highest mountains on all seven continents, becoming the first woman to complete the challenge known as the Seven Summits. Throughout her climbing career, Tabei defied expectations and stereotypes. She inspired athletes and women around the globe, giving speeches that encouraged others to follow their passions despite what society deemed acceptable. "There was never a question in my mind that I wanted to climb that mountain, no matter what other people said," Tabei remembered. Though the elements had been stacked against her, Junko Tabei came out on top.

# ALEX MORGAN

American soccer player Alex Morgan is an Olympic gold medalist and two-time FIFA (Fédération Internationale de Football Association) Women's World Cup champion. In 2016, one year after her first World Cup win, Morgan and four teammates filed a federal wage complaint against the U.S. Soccer Federation (USSF) on the grounds that the women's soccer team is paid less than the men's team, despite equal work. Following her second World Cup win in 2019, Morgan, alongside her two co-captains and 25 other team members, took the fight against gender discrimination to the next level by filing a federal lawsuit against the USSF.

## WHAT IS THE MOST IMPORTANT CHALLENGE FACING WOMEN TODAY?

**MORGAN:** There are so many challenges facing women today across the globe. One of the ones I feel is most important—in the workforce and in our personal lives—is that women need to feel unapologetic for going after their dreams. All too often, as women, we feel empowered to set goals for ourselves, but we don't feel comfortable aggressively trying to achieve them. We're shamed or criticized or perceived as "too ruthless." We need to feel comfortable and supported pursuing our dreams and unapologetic going after what we want.

## WHAT HAS BEEN A BREAKTHROUGH MOMENT IN YOUR LIFE?

**MORGAN:** My breakthrough moment was in March 2016 when four of my U.S. women's soccer teammates and I filed an official federal complaint [for equal pay and working conditions]. As of March 2019, [the case still hadn't received] a ruling—so 28 of us filed suit in the U.S. District Court against U.S. Soccer, seeking an end to the institutionalized gender discrimination that the women's team has endured for years. Regardless of the outcome, it will help bring the issue to people's attention. Regardless of the outcome, we will fight for equal pay, treatment, and working conditions.

## WHAT DO YOU THINK IS THE SINGLE MOST IMPORTANT CHANGE FOR WOMEN THAT NEEDS TO HAPPEN IN THE NEXT 10 YEARS?

**MORGAN:** The single most important change is getting more women in senior roles and putting women in positions of power where they can create policies that lead to long-lasting change.

## WHAT IS YOUR ADVICE TO YOUNG WOMEN TODAY?

**MORGAN:** Don't be discouraged in your journey. If people talk badly about you, if people say you can't achieve something, don't let it discourage you; let it drive you and steer you forward. No matter where you're at in life, or what you are trying to accomplish, people will always have their opinions. Listen to yourself, listen to your gut, and listen to the people in your life that you trust. Let your passions be your guide.

# SYLVIA EARLE

Dr. Sylvia Earle is a marine biologist, oceanographer, and explorer. She has led more than 100 expeditions—including the first team of women aquanauts to inhabit an underwater lab—and set the world untethered diving record at 1,250 feet (381 m) below the surface. Today, she continues her work as a National Geographic explorer-at-large, and founder of Mission Blue, a nonprofit organization that promotes ocean preservation.

## WHAT DO YOU THINK IS THE MOST IMPORTANT CHALLENGE FACING WOMEN TODAY?

 **EARLE:** I think the most important challenge is overcoming the habits that we've gotten into culturally—little boys are blue, little girls are pink; little boys do this and play with these kinds of toys, and little girls are encouraged in other directions.

## WHAT DO YOU THINK IS THE SINGLE MOST IMPORTANT CHANGE THAT NEEDS TO HAPPEN FOR WOMEN IN THE NEXT 10 YEARS?

 **EARLE:** Equal opportunity. To be judged on merit. The change is not just with how women are regarded by men, but how women regard themselves. You know, it starts with you.

## WHAT IS YOUR GREATEST STRENGTH?

 **EARLE:** Not giving up. Staying the course.

## WHAT ADVICE WOULD YOU GIVE TO YOUNG WOMEN TODAY?

 **EARLE:** The same advice I'd give to young men, I think. Find something that you love, that really makes your heart beat fast; even if you can't figure out how you could use that [skill] to make a living, make it a life. And be the best you can at whatever that is. Every person has power. At this point in history, we are endowed with superpowers because we have knowledge that could not exist before right about now. Our predecessors could not know what Earth looked like from afar, could not know how deep the ocean is or that life occurs there. So we've got an edge. My advice is to use that knowledge and to realize that we are at a pivotal point in both Earth history and human history. What we do or fail to do will determine whether we make it as a species on a planet that currently is in serious trouble.

## WHAT IS YOUR MOST CONSPICUOUS CHARACTER TRAIT?

 **EARLE:** Curiosity. Respect for life, all life, humans included.

THERE WAS A TIME WHEN CRITICS DISMISSED AMERICAN TENNIS PLAYER **BILLIE JEAN KING**'S TALENTS BECAUSE OF HER GENDER … UNTIL KING'S SKILLS AND DETERMINATION PROVED THEM WRONG.

King was the first woman to be named *Sports Illustrated's* **SPORTSPERSON OF THE YEAR.**

# SMASH STEREO

## THE BATTLE OF THE SEXES

In 1961, Billie Jean King (b. November 22, 1943) burst onto the international sports scene when she and her tennis partner became the youngest women to win the Wimbledon doubles title. Then in 1966, King won her first singles championship at Wimbledon, becoming the world's number one player in women's tennis. But for King, the battle was just beginning. Despite her victories and ranking, some people didn't take King seriously as an athlete due to her gender. One such critic was Bobby Riggs, a former number one men's tennis player. Riggs was familiar with King's talent and success but dismissed them. He declared that women's tennis was so inferior to men's tennis that he could beat the top female players—even though he was 55 years old and past his athletic prime. Riggs called King out specifically, but she initially turned him down. But after he played and embarrassed another female player in what he called "The Mother's Day Massacre," King decided to take him up on his challenge.

On September 20, 1973, millions of people were glued to their TV screens to watch the tennis showdown between King and Riggs. Was it true that women would always lose to men, like Riggs claimed? Riggs soon learned just how wrong his assumptions were: King dominated the match. She overtook Riggs, crushing any doubts about a woman's ability to be a tennis champion. With more than 90 million viewers, the battle became the most watched tennis match of all time—a record that holds to this day. Her victory inspired women across the world and opened doors for new professional women's tennis players.

## CONTINUING THE FIGHT

King's role as a champion for women continued off the court as well. In 1973, the same year as the Battle of the Sexes, she founded the Women's Tennis Association (WTA). Because of the WTA's advocacy, men and women now earn equal prize money at all four Grand Slam tournaments. King also later became one of the first prominent female athletes to openly identify as a lesbian and extended her advocacy to include LGBTQ+ rights. King's many victories—on and off the court—helped make people rethink what a woman's supposed limitations were, leading to long-lasting victories off the court and proving that women can achieve their goals, challenge the stereotypes that hold them back, and win.

### TRIUMPH LIKE KING!

**AIM HIGH**

From a young age, Billie Jean King wanted to be the number one tennis player in the world. Set yourself a goal, and figure out what the first step toward your dream would be. Then get to work!

**KEEP YOUR EYES ON THE PRIZE**

Sometimes someone just gets under your skin. But instead of getting angry, refocus your thoughts on your own goals—and don't let them knock you off your game.

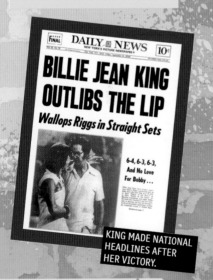

DAILY NEWS FINAL 10¢

**BILLIE JEAN KING OUTLIBS THE LIP**

*Wallops Riggs in Straight Sets*

6-4, 6-3, 6-3,
And No Love
For Bobby . . .

KING MADE NATIONAL HEADLINES AFTER HER VICTORY.

# TYPES

# GET THE GOLD

**SIMONE BILES** HOLDS THE MOST GOLD MEDALS OF ANY GYMNAST IN HISTORY, AND IS WIDELY CONSIDERED TO BE THE WORLD'S GREATEST GYMNAST.

Biles is known for **INVENTING NEW SKILLS** in practice.

## GOING FOR THE GOLD

Born in Columbus, Ohio, U.S.A., Simone Arianne Biles (b. March 14, 1997) found her calling in gymnastics while she was on a school field trip to a gym when she was only six years old. In 2013, Biles entered her first World Gymnastics Championships; she won the all-around title, becoming the first black woman to do so. But she was just getting started. She won four gold medals at the 2014 championships, and the next year Biles claimed a third consecutive all-around title victory, not to mention gold medals in balance beam, floor exercise, and the women's team competition. Over the next few years, Biles racked up a total of 20 championship medals. And she just kept going: In 2019, she became the first woman in history to land a triple-double on the floor exercise in competition. And that came the day after she'd stuck the landing on a history-making dismount, a double-twisting double somersault, during her balance beam routine! She also went on to win a record-tying sixth U.S. Championship and currently has two moves named after her in gymnastics' official Code of Points. Of Biles's current World Championship medals, 14 are gold, officially making her the number one gymnast in the world.

## A TRUE LEADER

Biles uses her talent and strength outside of competition, too. She has spoken out about the importance of supporting all female athletes, no matter their sport. She's also used her platform to discourage internet bullying. Like other black female athletes, Biles's appearance has been the target of criticism on social media. But she found a way to redirect the attention to her hard work and accomplishments. In early 2018, Biles disclosed that she, along with many of her teammates, was a victim of a former gymnastics doctor convicted of sexually abusing athletes. She has been an outspoken critic of the system that allowed the doctor to get away with his crimes. Biles's strength—both physical and mental—have established her as an elite athlete and inspiring leader for women everywhere. Who knows what records she'll break next?

# FIGHT LIKE A GIRL

## BORN TO BE A STAR

Angela Mao was born Mao Ching Ying in Taiwan on September 20, 1950, to Chinese opera stars. She began her own opera training at just five years old and also studied ballet and various martial arts, eventually earning her black belt in hapkido. When she was 20, Mao wanted to further her career and help support her family. Though she wasn't especially interested in becoming an actress, Hong Kong's movie industry was booming. So she made her way there and started seeking roles.

## LADY WHIRLWIND

At the time, women didn't typically get major parts in Hong Kong's movies. Instead, they were considered "decoration"—it was unusual for women to have speaking lines. But Mao refused to be reduced to a prop. Producer Raymond Chow discovered her during an opera performance, in which her martial arts skills drew his notice. Though many people warned Chow about casting a woman as a lead, claiming no one wanted to watch women in movies, Chow knew Mao was a special talent. The first film they made together, *Hapkido*, in 1972, was a hit.

Mao quickly became famous for her realistic fight scenes and precise hand-to-hand combat. Fans loved the way she took down bad guys twice her size, defeated crowds of attacking enemies, and skillfully whipped rivals with her long braid. She came to be known as "Lady Kung Fu" and "Lady Whirlwind" and made movies with martial arts legends Bruce Lee and Jackie Chan. She also made history: Mao was the first female kung fu star.

## A LEGENDARY LIFE

Despite her success, Mao had never aspired to be an actress, and after a brief career she retired to New York City with her husband and son. Even so, the legendary Lady Kung Fu lives on: Mao's work continues to inspire generations of stunt actors. When asked about her contribution to smashing gender stereotypes and paving the way for female kung fu artists, Mao said, "I just played myself. I am strong, and I am powerful."

KNOWN AS THE FIRST FEMALE KUNG FU STAR, **ANGELA MAO** STARRED IN MORE THAN 30 FILMS—EVEN THOUGH SHE NEVER AIMED TO BE A MOVIE STAR.

Mao went on to **OPEN SEVERAL CHINESE RESTAURANTS** in New York City.

CHAPTER **THREE**

# LITERA
# THE

THE PEABODY LIBRARY IN
BALTIMORE, MARYLAND

# TURE &
# ARTS

# BE ARTISTS!

**THE URGE TO CREATE ART IS UNIVERSALLY HUMAN—EVEN PEOPLE LIVING TENS OF THOUSANDS OF YEARS AGO PAINTED AND MADE JEWELRY.** But there was a time when girls were highly discouraged from becoming artists, musicians, or writers. That's right—even the world of literature and the arts isn't immune to gender bias. Women who create or perform have had to fight to be respected—a fight that continues to this day.

## WRITTEN OUT OF HISTORY

Famed writer Virginia Woolf once said, "I would venture to guess that Anon, who wrote so many poems without signing them, was often a woman." She was referring to the fact that female authors often chose to either publish anonymously or use a masculine-sounding pen name. Why would a woman publish something without putting her own name on it? Many felt they needed to change their name to be taken seriously as writers. And it isn't necessarily an outdated trend. Mary Ann Evans wrote under the name George Eliot in the 19th century, and Joanne Rowling went by just her initials—J. K. Rowling—when she wrote *Harry Potter* in the 1990s. Some female authors change their names in an effort to appeal to readers who, because of gender bias, would be more likely to read or admire books written by men. Across cultures and centuries, works written by men have been favored heavily. Men had the freedom to become respected authors, while society tended to dismiss the writings of women. Check out some of these odd reasons some people believe that "women can't write."

**MYTH #1:** THERE ARE WAY MORE **FAMOUS MALE AUTHORS,** SO MEN MUST BE BETTER AT WRITING.

**FALSE!** This statement assumes that the playing field for male and female authors has been equal all along, and that women have had the same opportunities for their work to be published under their real names. But unfortunately, this simply isn't the case. For many centuries in many areas of the world, women were denied equal access to education, which included learning to read and write—not to mention being allowed to work. As a result, is it any wonder that men came to dominate this field?

## UNEQUAL OPPORTUNITIES

Gender bias in the arts isn't limited to literature. Of the 600 songs that were on the Billboard Hot 100 music charts between 2012 and 2017, women performed only 22 percent. That means only 132 of the most popular songs in a five-year span were by a woman. And just 12 percent of those songs had at least one female writer or music producer. (That's only 72 songs.)

Similarly, female visual artists throughout history have rarely been given equal opportunities and often have been overlooked. Western women were largely not allowed to engage in art studies until the 16th century, and even then they were often barred from many classes. On the rare occasion women did get to paint, it was considered a bit scandalous. In fact, the only women who seemed free to paint without repercussion were nuns in monasteries. Although the number of female artists has greatly increased since then, an imbalance in recognition still exists today. Women are the subjects of many pieces found in museums, but they are less likely to be the creators of the art on display. A recent survey of 18 respected museums found that only 13 percent of featured artists were female. But women are working to change the game. Not only are more female artists being recognized today, artists from history who were either unknown or lost are being rediscovered.

The creative works of women have been—and will continue to be—vital to the way everyone experiences culture. In this chapter, you'll meet women who are game changers in the worlds of art, literature, and performance. They all prove that girls create great art.

**MYTH #2:** WOMEN ONLY WRITE ABOUT **ROMANCE,** AND ROMANCE IS BORING.

**FALSE!** Historically the romance genre has largely been written and read by women. Romance novels were deemed more acceptable and in line with expectations for women; they were once considered the only way female writers could break into the world of popular literature. As gender roles have shifted and become less rigid, the idea that women can only write romance has faded. From science fiction to horror to Westerns, women are doing it all. Though there's nothing wrong with a good romance novel—whether written by a woman or a man!

**MYTH #3:** READING IS **BAD FOR WOMEN.**

**FALSE!** Okay, this one isn't widely believed these days, but people in 18th-century England really thought that novels were bad for women. (To set the record straight: It's totally untrue!) They believed excessive novel reading had bad effects on a woman's "mental system"—that reading altered women's minds and even stopped them from being able to distinguish fiction from reality. And the same misguided ideas were applied to women who wrote novels.

**FRIDA KAHLO** WAS A RENOWNED ARTIST WHOSE WORK IS CELEBRATED FOR ITS VIVID IMAGERY AND CELEBRATION OF MEXICAN HERITAGE AND FEMALE IDENTITY.

Of Kahlo's 143 paintings, 55 are **SELF-PORTRAITS.**

# MAKE MASTER

## HEALING THROUGH ART

Born in Coyoacán, Mexico, Frida Kahlo (July 6, 1907–July 13, 1954) contracted polio at the age of six. The disease left her frail and confined to bed for nine months, which was when she first began to dabble in painting. But when she recovered, Kahlo put art aside and focused on studying human anatomy. At 15, she became one of the few female students accepted into the National Preparatory School's prestigious premedical program. While at school, Kahlo became more active in politics and met her future husband, muralist Diego Rivera.

But a bus accident when she was 18 left Kahlo seriously injured with a shattered pelvis and multiple fractures along her back, collarbone, and ribs. She required dozens of operations and more than a year of bed rest. During her extended recovery time, she remembered her childhood love of painting.

## DEFYING EXPECTATIONS

Painting allowed Kahlo to work through her pain and experience the world despite being confined to bed. As she recovered, she began to use her art to explore her own identity. She exaggerated her unibrow and light mustache in

KAHLO PAINTING A PORTRAIT

self-portraits. She also explored her physical pain in her work.

Kahlo went on to marry Rivera, and the pair spent the late 1920s and 1930s traveling across Mexico and the United States. All the while, Kahlo perfected her skills, gained inspiration from her travels, and developed a unique personal style. She returned home with a strengthened love for her country and a determination to represent Mexican culture and national identity. In 1939, Kahlo moved to Paris, where she continued to sell her work and built friendships with artists like Pablo Picasso and Marcel Duchamp. She reached new heights in the art world when she became the first Mexican artist to be featured in the Louvre's collection.

## LONGSTANDING LEGACY

Although she had achieved notable success for a female artist at the time, Kahlo's work was often overshadowed by other male artists. It took the feminist movement of the 1970s—two decades after her death—for her to be recognized as an artist who celebrated herself, portrayed her own pain, and explored femininity. Kahlo came to be considered a creative feminist icon. Her family home is now a museum, and both she and her work continue to inspire and challenge ideas about identity, strength, beauty, and worth.

## CREATE LIKE KAHLO!

### USE ART AS AN OUTLET

Although Kahlo is a globally renowned name today, she painted first and foremost for herself, and to get through tough times. Above all, remember that your art is for you and that it can be a great tool when things get rough.

# PIECES

# INFLUENCE NATIONS

AN ANCIENT CARVING SHOWING ENHEDUANNA

CARVING OF THE GODDESS INANNA

**ENHEDUANNA** WAS A MESOPOTAMIAN PRINCESS AND PRIESTESS. SHE ALSO HAPPENS TO BE THE WORLD'S FIRST AUTHOR AND POET KNOWN BY NAME.

"Enheduanna" may have been an official **SUMERIAN TITLE.**

## FROM PRINCESS TO HIGH PRIESTESS

Sargon the Great had just conquered the entirety of Mesopotamia, an ancient area covering modern-day Iraq and parts of Iran, Syria, and Turkey. He came from a region known as Akkad to the north and now ruled all the way south to a region called Sumer. It would be a tall order to unify the Akkadians and the newly conquered Sumerians. Sargon needed someone he could rely on, someone who was a skilled politician: his daughter, Enheduanna (circa 2285 B.C.). Though historians today disagree on whether Enheduanna was really Sargon's daughter (as well as whether "Enheduanna" was her title or her name), it is clear that she played a vital role in the empire.

Sargon installed Enheduanna as high priestess in the ancient city of Ur. There, she worked to unify the Akkadians and the Sumerians under one religion by composing poetic hymns to Inanna, the Sumerian goddess of love and war. These hymns, which would have spread throughout the empire, elevated Inanna from a simple local goddess to the "Queen of Heaven," making her the most popular deity in Mesopotamia. They also created a new, united culture that helped keep peace in the region. But Enheduanna's job was not without its problems: At one point, she was overthrown by a Sumerian rebel and forced into exile, which she recorded in her writings. The powerful princess fought back against the coup, though, and she was restored to her position as high priestess.

## LEGENDARY SKILLS

In addition to her accomplished work as a politician and priestess, Enheduanna was also a gifted poet. She is best known today for three surviving hymns she wrote to Inanna. But Enheduanna also wrote poetry for herself—42 of her personal poems have survived. These poems, which detail her fears, hopes, reactions to various events, and more, offer fantastic insight into life more than 4,000 years ago. They had a lasting cultural effect and are thought to have possibly inspired parts of both the Hebrew Bible and the poet Homer's works. Her poems were read for centuries after her death; a surviving disc honoring her was found to have been made hundreds of years after she lived. Today Enheduanna is the world's oldest known author and poet.

# MASTER A CRAFT

A BUST CREATED BY LEWIS

## TOO WILD

Life for Mary Edmonia Lewis (circa July 4, 1844–September 17, 1907) was challenging from the start. Born to a black father and an Ojibwe mother, she faced difficulties because her parents were from two different marginalized groups. Lewis was orphaned at a young age and went to live with relatives in the Ojibwe tribe. She attended primary school but was rejected after three years for being too "wild." Even so, a determined Lewis made her way to Oberlin College in Oberlin, Ohio, U.S.A., where she studied sculpture. Again, she was met with discrimination. Lewis was wrongly accused of poisoning two of her roommates and of theft. Though she would later be cleared of the charges, a mob descended on Lewis and beat her over the accusations. Lewis left Oberlin and moved to Boston, Massachusetts, U.S.A., where she began her life as a sculptor.

## TAKING RISKS

In Boston, Lewis studied with local sculptors. She created and sold medallions and busts of famous abolitionists and Civil War heroes. With the money she earned from selling her sculptures, Lewis decided to take a great risk: travel alone to Italy. She settled in Rome, learned Italian, and began studying classical methods of sculpture-making. Her work included something new, though, which set her apart from classical sculptors: her own heritage. Lewis carved stunning and moving depictions of stories that were deeply familiar to her. She created a powerful work portraying a newly freed black couple titled "Forever Free," and she decided to take yet another risk with it. She shipped the sculpture to Boston, to the home of famed abolitionist Samuel Sewall, hoping he might find a buyer for it. Sewall was surprised when "Forever Free" arrived, but he did follow through with selling the piece. Buyers began to take note of Lewis's exceptional talents, and her work was soon in high demand. By 1876, Lewis was of such renown that she was invited to participate in the United States' first official world's fair. Lewis had reached levels of success nearly unheard of for someone born into such difficult circumstances. Because her determination was so great and her talent so extraordinary, Lewis managed to overcome enormously stacked odds to become the first internationally recognized sculptor of black or Native descent.

**EDMONIA LEWIS** BECAME THE FIRST INTERNATIONALLY FAMOUS BLACK NATIVE AMERICAN SCULPTOR.

Lewis's work can be viewed today at New York's **METROPOLITAN MUSEUM OF ART.**

# WELL-WRITTEN WOMEN

## TIRED OF READING ABOUT DAMSELS IN DISTRESS?

**Women today are making history as authors, artists, and actresses.** But it's important to recognize the great female role models depicted in works of art as well as those behind them! After all, some of the most influential people you meet can be the ones you find in your favorite books, movies, and TV shows. By portraying women as talented and multi-layered people, authors and artists can help shatter stereotypes and inspire others. Check out some of the fantastic female characters who represent women in fiction.

### FA MULAN
In the Disney movie *Mulan*, Fa Mulan (based on the Chinese piece titled *The Ballad of Mulan*) refuses to wait for some-one else to save her. In fact, she insists on saving her father—and all of China—from the attacking Huns by sneaking into the Imperial Army disguised as a man.

### PRINCESS SHURI
Shuri, princess of Wakanda and younger sister of King T'Challa (aka Black Panther), is undoubtedly a hero and an inspiration in her own right. Both an inventor and a skilled fighter, Shuri is incredibly loyal to her family and to Wakanda and will defend her people to the end.

### LIEUTENANT UHURA

A communications officer serving on the USS *Enterprise* in the *Star Trek* television series and movies, Lieutenant Uhura is fluent in Swahili and specializes in languages and secret communications. Aside from being talented and intelligent in her own right, Uhura's character broke boundaries with the original casting of Nichelle Nichols, one of the first black actors to be featured in a major role on television.

## WRITE HER WELL!

**What makes for a well-written character?** Forget that she's a girl! Instead of defining characters by gender, focus instead on what makes them unique—their interests, background, goals, and secrets. The best female characters are complex, well-rounded individuals—just like any other people out there.

### AMERICA CHAVEZ

America Chavez, a Latina lesbian character, is an independent superhero with the powers of super-strength, superspeed, teleportation, and flight. Originally part of the Young Avengers, Chavez now spends her time defending Earth as a member of the West Coast Avengers.

### HERMIONE GRANGER

Hermione Granger from J. K. Rowling's beloved Harry Potter series is an inspiration for smart people everywhere. She proudly excels in class and on assignments. Granger uses her knowledge and logic to solve mysteries and demonstrates curiosity, compassion, and courage in the face of discrimination against her non-magic family.

# WRITE

**PHILLIS WHEATLEY** LIVED THROUGH THE TRIALS OF SLAVERY, YET WENT ON TO BECOME BOTH AN ACCOMPLISHED POET AND THE FIRST BLACK FEMALE PUBLISHED WRITER.

STATUE OF WHEATLEY IN BOSTON, MASSACHUSETTS

## FORCED INTO SLAVERY

Born around 1753 in Gambia, West Africa, Phillis Wheatley (whose birth name is unknown) was eight years old when she was captured by slave traders and brought to America. She was sold at a slave auction in Boston, Massachusetts, to a family that renamed her Phillis after the slave ship on which she was forced to cross the Atlantic Ocean. Wheatley was made to perform maid duties and was not allowed to leave the property or make decisions of her own. However, she was taught to read and given an education, unlike most slaves.

## A TALENTED POET

After only 16 months of schooling, she could read the Bible, Greek and Latin classics, and British literature. By age 12, she had developed a love for writing poetry and her first published work appeared a year later in the *Newport Mercury*, a local paper. Wheatley found fame after publishing "An Elegiac Poem, on the Death of the Celebrated Divine ... George Whitefield." English Countess of Huntingdon offered her sponsorship, and Wheatley journeyed to London—in the forced accompaniment of the Wheatleys' son—to publish her first collection of poems, *Poems on Various Subjects, Religious and Moral*. It was the first ever published book written by a black woman in America. To prove who the author was, the book included her portrait and a foreword signed by distinguished Bostonians like John Hancock. Soon after publishing the book, Wheatley was freed from slavery.

## A VOICE FOR MANY

Wheatley's poetry celebrated her devotion to her religion and pride in her African heritage. At a time when the shameful practice of slavery divided many in the United States, Wheatley's work found an audience among both black and white people. White slaveholders used her poems to try to convince the enslaved people they owned to convert to Christianity, while abolitionists viewed her work as an example of the intellectual abilities of people of color. Despite the appropriation of her work by slave

# WITH POWER

AN ILLUSTRATION OF WHEATLEY THAT APPEARED ON THE FRONT PAGE OF HER BOOK OF POEMS

owners, Wheatley was outspoken about her opposition to slavery and often denounced it in her writing.

Wheatley lived her life as a free woman, writing and marrying a free black man from Boston named John Peters in 1778. But the couple struggled, and Wheatley worked as a scrubwoman to support her children. The family endured the deaths of three children in the course of just six years, and Wheatley died during childbirth in December 1784. Though she never had enough money to publish a second book of poetry, the intelligence and thoughtfulness of her existing work lives on and inspires. Her contribution to American literature helped progress the abolitionist movement and inspires the fight for equal rights centuries later.

**OPRAH WINFREY** IS A HISTORY-MAKING AMERICAN TALK SHOW HOST, ACTRESS, PHILANTHROPIST, AND MEDIA EXECUTIVE.

## A CHALLENGING CHILDHOOD

Oprah Winfrey (b. January 29, 1954) may be a household name today, but her early life was challenging. Her parents separated soon after she was born, and Winfrey shifted between living with her mother and grandmother. She suffered from abuse at the hands of family members and lived in poverty, wearing clothes made of potato sacks to school. Desperate, Winfrey attempted to run away from home when she was 14, but she was sent to a juvenile detention center. At age 17, Winfrey was able to live with her father in Nashville, Tennessee, U.S.A. Supported by his encouragement, Winfrey became a school superstar and even got a job with a local radio station.

## CONQUERING THE AIRWAVES

Winfrey now seemed unstoppable. She became the first black woman news anchor at WTVF-TV 5, a local Nashville station, and her rise continued when she moved to Chicago,

# BECOME AN ICON

Illinois, U.S.A., to be the host of a morning news program called *AM Chicago*. Within a few short months, the show had jumped from last place in the ratings all the way to the top. It wasn't long before *AM Chicago* was renamed and relaunched as *The Oprah Winfrey Show* in 1986.

*The Oprah Winfrey Show*, usually referred to as *Oprah*, quickly became the number one talk show in America. Oprah used her wits and talent to spin her hit show into even more opportunities. By the time the last *Oprah* show aired in 2011, she was far more than a talk show host. Winfrey is an award-winning actress and producer of movies and TV projects; she co-founded a women's television network, built her own production studio, and became the first woman to own and produce her own talk show. The girl from Mississippi who had once worn potato sacks to school had created a business empire and become the first black female billionaire.

### PAYING IT FORWARD

Winfrey has spearheaded many philanthropy projects around the world, including a girls' school she founded in South Africa. She has touched the lives of millions of people and continues to make a lasting impact on those she encounters.

Winfrey is the **FIRST BLACK WOMAN** to receive the Golden Globe's Cecil B. DeMille Award for outstanding contributions to the world of entertainment.

## WHAT DO YOU THINK IS THE BIGGEST CHALLENGE FOR WOMEN TODAY?

**WINFREY:** [Equality] continues to be our biggest challenge, and understanding that as an individual born on the planet, as a woman citizen, you have a right to that. When you understand that, you know that you belong here and you are not suffering from what I think is one of the most discouraging things: not feeling that you're worthy.

## WHAT KIND OF ADVICE WOULD YOU GIVE TO A YOUNG WOMAN TODAY?

**WINFREY:** The advice is always the same: the truth is the truth is the truth is the truth, and nothing works other than being the truth of yourself. I have a girls' school, I have 191 girls in college right now, all at various stages calling me about one thing or another. Whether it's a boyfriend problem, a money problem, or a trying-to-figure-out-what-I-want-to-do-with-my-life problem, my message is always: Get still enough to understand and hear the truth speak through you. The voices of the world will drown out your true voice if you allow them to. But if you can get still enough, it's always there. Every question that you have, an answer to it is always there. It can be hard to hear that voice if you're listening to everybody else.

## WHAT DO YOU THINK IS THE MOST IMPORTANT CHANGE THAT NEEDS TO HAPPEN FOR WOMEN IN THE NEXT 10 YEARS?

**WINFREY:** I think that everything starts with you. I love this phrase now of people getting woke because I've been speaking to people awakening themselves for years, and I know that everything essentially begins with you—then your connection to other people and your willingness to use that power for something greater than yourself.

## WHAT DO YOU THINK IS YOUR GREATEST STRENGTH?

**WINFREY:** No question, it's connection to other people. I think one of my greatest strengths is being fully present so that in any given moment, in any conversation with anybody, I can put myself in the space of where they are in that moment and meet them where they are.

# GIRLS WHO GEEK OUT

**"GIRLS DON'T PLAY VIDEO GAMES."**

**"OH, SHE'S JUST A FAKE GEEK GIRL."**

**"GIRLS DON'T READ COMIC BOOKS."**

**Sound familiar? For years, people have made incorrect assumptions about what girls might be interested in** and have tried to push them out of "geek spaces" by insisting that women lack talent or are only pretending to be interested in "nerdy" topics. Many women even have to deal with online bullies who harass and threaten them. But of course, plenty of girls do love nerdy things. Studies show that 45 percent of video game players and 46.7 percent of comic book fans are female. Happily, women are now building supportive and inclusive geek communities together. Check out some of these amazing girls who geek out!

**MARJANE SATRAPI, Graphic novel author**
Born in Iran, Marjane Satrapi is an artist and author. In her award-winning graphic novels *Persepolis* and *Persepolis 2*, she depicts her childhood growing up in Iran during the Iranian revolution in 1979. The books have received critical acclaim for their representation of strong women in the Middle East.

## JOIN IN THE FUN

**Tired of sitting on the sidelines watching someone else play a game or create a costume?** The best way to join in is to become part of a community. See if there is a local gaming group you can sign up with, or have an adult help you find a positive and welcoming online community that gives advice on cosplay. Dive in, ask questions, and have fun!

## ARIGON STARR,
### Musician, actress, author, and artist

Arigon Starr is an enrolled member of the Kickapoo tribe who grew up singing and acting. In 2007, Starr debuted a radio comedy series about a Native American superhero called *Super Indian*. Using her artistic talents, she went on to turn *Super Indian* into an online comic series and graphic novel. Her work was also recently featured in *Moonshot: The Indigenous Comics Collection, Volume 1*.

## ARIELL JOHNSON,
### Comic book store owner

A self-described geek, Ariell Johnson created Amalgam Comics & Coffeehouse in Philadelphia, Pennsylvania, U.S.A. It is the first comic book shop owned by a black woman on the United States' East Coast. Amalgam is committed to representation and inclusion and features a variety of comics by women from different backgrounds.

## "FAKE GEEK GIRLS"

**Why would anyone believe that women don't belong in the geek world?** It turns out, the fault lies with marketing! Early comic books from the 1940s were targeted at both men and women as inspiring stories to read during wartime. But in the 1950s, a trend toward more conservative gender roles led companies to market superhero comic books toward men only. Similarly, early video games like Pong were billed as family games, but after a market crash in 1983, gaming companies decided to target a narrower audience to boost sales. Their chosen group? Teenage boys. Over time, all this targeted marketing convinced people that only boys and men were interested in comics and video games.

# TELL
# STORIES

**ERIKA LARSEN** IS A NATIONAL GEOGRAPHIC EXPLORER AND PHOTOGRAPHER WHO DOCUMENTS COMMUNITIES OF PEOPLE WITH CLOSE CULTURAL TIES TO NATURE.

The Sami people have been inhabiting Arctic regions for more than 3,000 YEARS!

## THE MAGIC OF PHOTOGRAPHY

Erika Larsen (b. November 15, 1976) fell in love with photography while she was holding a picture of the planet Saturn. Though Saturn is far away and untouchable, the photo in her hand—which was taken by the Hubble telescope—allowed Larsen to experience it for herself. The image inspired Larsen to pursue photography not only as an art but also as a tool through which distant things and experiences could be made real and accessible to people. Larsen's family encouraged her to pursue her dreams, and she began to travel and document the world around her with her camera. She embraced the idea that a photographer is a story-teller, incorporating writing, video, and audio into her work.

## SHARING EXPERIENCES

Larsen is perhaps best known for documenting the lives of the Sami, an indigenous people that live in parts of the Arctic Circle. She spent more than four years living with Sami reindeer herders and documenting their daily lives. In 2001, Larsen published a piece on the herders in *National Geographic* magazine, sharing her experience with the world. Larsen went on to document the importance of horses in Native American cultures by visiting communities across the country, including the Yakama, Navajo, and Cheyenne Nations. Larsen continues to work closely with National Geographic, traveling and learning more about how animals and natural resources affect human lives and cultures. Her photographs allow audiences to connect with cultures across the globe and to learn more about each other and themselves. Each project she takes on requires dedication and presents its own unique challenges, but Larsen remains inspired by her passion to explore the connections humans feel with nature.

Larsen's photography has been displayed in the Smithsonian National Portrait Gallery in Washington, D.C., the Fotografiska museum in Sweden, the Reggio Calabria National Archaeological Museum in Italy, and at Visa pour l'Image in Perpignan, France. Her work offers an important tool for understanding interactions between humans and nature and helps share these experiences with audiences across the globe.

THE HEYDAR ALIYEV CENTER IN BAKU, AZERBAIJAN, DESIGNED BY HADID

# PAVE THE WAY

## MAKING HER MARK

The world of architecture is not known for being welcoming to women. In the late 1800s, designs from the first known female architects were criticized for their "daintiness" and weren't taken seriously. Even today female architects are often overlooked in favor of their male peers. But Zaha Hadid (October 31, 1950–March 31, 2016) was determined to make her mark on the world, and she was determined to do it through architecture.

Born in Baghdad, Iraq, Hadid studied mathematics and architecture before establishing her own firm, Zaha Hadid Architects. It wasn't long before Hadid began to win competitions, including the design for a private center in Hong Kong that she titled "The Peak." But "The Peak" was never built, and critics began to label Hadid a "paper architect," meaning a designer whose ideas work only on paper and can't be built in real life. The criticism intensified when museums began to display her designs as art. People claimed that Hadid made pretty drawings, but that she wasn't a real architect. She was attacked in a way that male architects never typically were, raising the question of whether she was being targeted because of her gender. Hadid decided to prove these critics wrong.

## BECOMING THE QUEEN

In 1993, Hadid's first building, the Vitra Fire Station, was completed. After that, she became unstoppable, gaining fame for her trademark sharp angles and flowing planes. In 2003, Hadid made history when she became the first woman to design an American museum. In 2004, she made history again by becoming the first woman to win the Pritzker Architecture Prize, a prestigious international award. She didn't stop there. She went on to win a Stirling Prize from the Royal Institute of British Architects (RIBA) in both 2010 and 2011, became the first woman to win the London Design Museum's Design of the Year in 2015, and the first woman to win a RIBA gold medal in 2016. Hadid passed away suddenly later that year, leaving behind many unfinished projects. But she had accomplished her goal, quite literally making her mark on the world through her futuristic, fluid designs. She had also paved the way for future women in architecture to achieve their own goals.

**ZAHA HADID** WAS A WORLD-RENOWNED ARCHITECT AND BECAME THE FIRST WOMAN TO RECEIVE THE PRESTIGIOUS PRITZKER ARCHITECTURE PRIZE.

Hadid's architecture firm continues to complete her designs, including the 2022 WORLD CUP STADIUM in Qatar.

**MARIA TALLCHIEF** WAS THE FIRST NATIVE AMERICAN WOMAN TO BECOME A PRIMA BALLERINA IN A BALLET COMPANY. SHE IS CONSIDERED ONE OF THE GREATEST AMERICAN DANCERS OF ALL TIME.

Tallchief received the **NATIONAL MEDAL OF ARTS** from the National Endowment for the Arts in 1999.

# TAKE CENTER

## A NATURAL DANCER

Elizabeth Marie Tall Chief, or Tallchief, as she was later known, (January 24, 1925–April 11, 2013) was born on an Osage Nation reservation in Oklahoma, U.S.A. Her grandmother often took her to ceremonial tribal dances as a child, and she began ballet at age three. Her gift for dancing was impossible to miss, and when she turned eight, Tallchief's family moved to Beverly Hills, California, U.S.A., to find better training opportunities for her. By 12 years old she was studying under a famous Russian ballerina, and at 15 she performed her first solo at the Hollywood Bowl in Los Angeles. As soon as she graduated high school, 17-year-old Tallchief moved to New York City, aiming to earn a spot with a major ballet company.

## DANCING PAST DISCRIMINATION

But in New York, Tallchief struggled to join a company; she encountered prejudice and discrimination against her Native heritage. She had faced racism in the past, particularly during middle school. But Tallchief hadn't given up as a middle schooler, and she didn't now. Finally, in 1942, she was offered a spot as an understudy with the Ballet Russe de Monte Carlo company. The Russian ballerinas in the company looked down on American dancers and often picked on Tallchief. She was pressured to change her last name to something more Russian-sounding. She refused to abandon her Osage heritage, but compromised by calling herself "Maria." Tallchief had her big break later that year when she replaced a lead ballerina during a performance. She performed beautifully, earning high praise from critics for her first foray into the spotlight.

## PRIMA BALLERINA

When the famous choreographer George Balanchine took over the Ballet Russe in 1944, he promoted Tallchief to the leading ballerina's understudy. Balanchine and Tallchief soon married and left for Paris, where Tallchief became the first American woman to dance in the Paris Opera Ballet. On returning to the United States, Balanchine formed his own company, the New York City Ballet. There, Tallchief became the star female dancer—the prima ballerina. She wasn't only the first Native American prima ballerina, she was the first prima ballerina in all of the United States. For 18 years she dazzled as one of the most talented ballerinas in the world.

After retiring from performing in 1965, Tallchief founded a ballet school and worked as artistic director of the Chicago City Ballet. She was inducted into the National Women's Hall of Fame in 1996. She was also honored by the Osage Nation, earning the title Wa-Xthe-Thomba, or "Woman of Two Worlds." Tallchief is still celebrated for her incredible talents, as well as her ability to break down barriers.

TALLCHIEF IN HER HOMETOWN

# STAGE

# CHIMAMANDA NGOZI ADICHIE

Born and raised in Nigeria, Chimamanda Ngozi Adichie is an award-winning author whose works have received international acclaim. She has composed works on the Nigeria-Biafra War, which took place in her home country from 1967 to 1970, as well as on race, gender equality and feminism, and other social, political, and economic issues shaping today's world. She is an outspoken advocate for women's rights and continues to create moving works in the form of short stories, essays, novels, and more.

## WHAT DO YOU THINK IS THE MOST IMPORTANT THING THAT NEEDS TO CHANGE FOR WOMEN IN THE NEXT FEW YEARS?

 We need to have more women in positions of decision-making—politically, economically, in every way. More women's representation will result in more diverse decisions that incorporate women's experiences. I don't think having women in positions of power means that the world is going to be perfect or that conflict will be eradicated. It just means that the concerns of half of the world's population will finally be center stage.

## WHEN YOU LOOK BACK THROUGH YOUR LIFE, IS THERE SOMETHING THAT YOU WOULD CONSIDER A BREAKTHROUGH MOMENT?

 I think it was when I was nine years old, in the third grade, and I remember this very clearly. My teacher had said that the child with the best results on the test that she gave would be the prefect [a student with more authority]. So I got the best result—and then she said, "Oh, I forgot to mention, it has to be a boy." I just thought, Why? It would make sense to have said the class prefect has to be the child with the best grades or the child with some sort of useful skill. But to me, the idea that this position in the classroom was reserved for somebody simply by being born [male]—that was just strange. So my sense of righteous indignation flared up and I said to my teacher, "That makes no sense."

## WHAT ADVICE WOULD YOU GIVE TO YOUNG WOMEN TODAY?

 Don't apologize. I think women are generally socialized to be apologetic—just for existing, in many ways, or for having opinions that are not mainstream. Girls are socialized to think that they need to be liked, and it makes them pretend to be what they're not. I would say to young women, Don't do it. Because it's not worth it. Because if somebody likes you because you are pretending, they don't really like you. They like a different, false version of you. It sounds simplistic, but I think it's quite difficult, considering all the messages that society gives young women.

# ROXANE GAY

Roxane Gay is a *New York Times* best-selling author whose work explores identity, race, gender, and more. Her essays and collections provide insight into her own experiences as a survivor of rape and disordered eating, as well as her battles against bigotry as a bisexual black woman. She also continues to make waves in the comic book industry as the author of Marvel's *Black Panther: World of Wakanda* comic book series. She is currently a visiting professor at Yale University.

## WHAT DO YOU THINK IS YOUR GREATEST STRENGTH?

 My greatest strength is to communicate complicated ideas, and to recognize that points of view I disagree with still have value.

## WHAT IS YOUR MOST NOTABLE CHARACTER TRAIT?

 My opinionated nature.

## WHAT ADVICE WOULD YOU GIVE TO YOUNG WOMEN TODAY?

 I think that young women have to be able to stand up for themselves and advocate for themselves without fear. I think it's important for young women to embrace their ambition and to know their worth and to ask for it.

## WHAT WAS YOUR BREAKTHROUGH MOMENT?

 I think my big breakthrough moment was really when *Bad Feminist*, my first essay collection, was published and I realized that [others related to] my way of seeing and discussing the world.

## WHAT DO YOU THINK ARE THE GREATEST CHALLENGES FACING WOMEN TODAY?

 Things are complicated for women right now in that things have gotten better, but some rights we had hoped would become inalienable are no longer inalienable. So, I think reproductive rights and equal pay are the two greatest challenges.

**GUAN DAOSHENG** IS OFTEN NAMED AS THE MOST FAMOUS FEMALE PAINTER IN CHINESE HISTORY. SHE DEFIED EXPECTATIONS BY EXCELLING IN AREAS OF ART TRADITIONALLY RESERVED FOR MEN.

An explanation of Daosheng's artistic technique is still considered a classic piece **SEVEN HUNDRED YEARS LATER.**

# PAINT A NEW

## A PRIVILEGED START

In 1262, during the Yuan dynasty (1206–1368), Guan Daosheng (circa 1262–1319) was born to wealthy parents in Huzhou, China. Though women typically held traditional, domestic roles in that era, Daosheng's father encouraged her education more than her home-making skills. When Daosheng was around 27 years old, she entered into an arranged marriage with Zhao Mengfu, an artist and bureau-crat. Together, they traveled across much of China, painting temple murals and conducting business along the way. Their journey allowed Daosheng to see and experience much of her country beyond her home, which was very unusual for most women of the time. But Daosheng was accustomed to unconventional ways, and she was just beginning to make waves.

## UNCONVENTIONAL ART

When the emperor invited the nation's most talented artists and scholars to his court, Daosheng and her husband accepted the emperor's offer and moved to the nation's capi-tal. At this time in China's history, most women who worked in creative fields were actresses, not painters, so Daosheng continued to stand out. Not only that, she painted in

traditionally masculine styles, includ-ing bamboo painting, which depicted detailed prints of bamboo plants. Because bamboo was a hearty and tough plant, it was often considered "manly." But Daosheng amazed everyone with her skill, including critics who were impressed that her bamboo paintings were just as good—and frequently better—than many painted by famous male artists. Daosheng even expanded acceptable styles of bamboo paint-ing by depicting bamboo as part of the landscape rather than by itself. She also incorporated calligraphy and poetry into her paintings.

## HIGH PRAISE

Daosheng's work was highly praised by the emperor and continued to gain admirers. Some of her pieces even received the imperial seal. Daosheng went on to earn the title Wei Kuo fu-jen or "Lady of the Wei Kingdom." After her death, her work continued to inspire, and Daosheng is revered as one of China's greatest artists. One of her most famous pieces is "Ten Thousand Bamboo Poles in Cloudy Mist," which is the earliest surviving example of art created by a woman in China. Thanks to her willingness to buck tradition and share her talent, Daosheng is still celebrated to this day.

## CREATE LIKE DAOSHENG!

### MAKE YOUR OWN RULES

Bamboo painting may have been thought of as "mascu-line," but Daosheng was never one to be limited by tradi-tional roles or expectations. By breaking society's gender roles, she reinvented what it meant to be a painter in China during the Yuan dynasty. Art is a great place to push the envelope—how can you use creativity to break down stereotypes?

### TRAVEL FOR ART

The traveling Daosheng did opened her eyes to life in other parts of her country. Experiencing new people, places, and things can expand your perspective—both in life and in what you create.

A PAINTING OF A BAMBOO GROVE ATTRIBUTED TO DAOSHENG

# PICTURE

# SING OUT

## BORN TO SING

Born Eunice Kathleen Waymon, Nina Simone (February 21, 1933–April 21, 2003) played piano exceptionally from an early age. She also encountered prejudice. During Simone's first piano recital, her parents were removed from their seats in the front row and sent to the back to "make room" for white people. Young Simone refused to play until her parents were given their rightful seats back, and the event marked the beginning of Simone's lifelong fight for equality through her music.

Simone studied classical music at Juilliard, a prestigious music conservatory in New York City. Despite her talent, she faced heavy bias as a woman and a person of color. When she later applied to the Curtis Institute of Music in Philadelphia, Pennsylvania, U.S.A. and was rejected, Simone attributed the decision to racial bias. But she continued her training and finally broke out shortly after she started singing in 1954 and adopted her stage name Nina Simone. A few years later, her version of the song "I Loves You, Porgy" became a smash hit. She had found success, but Simone was ready to use her music to achieve something more.

## USING HER VOICE

In the 1960s, the American civil rights movement was in full swing. Simone was friends with leaders of the movement, including Martin Luther King, Jr., Malcolm X, and artists such as Langston Hughes and Lorraine Hansberry. Simone had personally endured the racism that the civil rights movement sought to end, and she was keenly aware of how racism and violence affected others. So Simone put her talents to work and began to write protest songs, performing them at civil rights demonstrations. Songs such as "Backlash Blues" and "I Wish I Knew How It Would Feel to Be Free" were not easy for white audiences to hear. Simone faced backlash from people who thought her music was too harsh and angry. But for many people, her songs were revolutionary. They became key parts of the civil rights movement, inspiring countless activists.

Simone eventually retired to Barbados but continued to travel the world and sing. Though she passed away in 2003, her legacy endures: Countless artists have covered her songs and credit her as an inspiration to use music as a tool for change.

**NINA SIMONE** WAS AN AMERICAN PERFORMER, SONGWRITER, PIANIST, AND CIVIL RIGHTS ACTIVIST KNOWN FOR HER SOULFUL VOICE AND MUSICAL STYLE.

Simone came to be known as the **"HIGH PRIESTESS OF SOUL"** for her powerful and passionate voice.

# GET LAUGHS

## COMEDY QUEEN

Ellen Lee DeGeneres (b. January 26, 1958) seemed to fall into comedy almost by accident. In the late 1970s, DeGeneres began performing a comedy routine for a group of friends. It was a hit, and she eventually fielded requests for her routine from local coffeehouses. Soon, she was traveling through the United States on the comedy club circuit. DeGeneres finally got her big break in 1994, when she got to star in her own television series, *Ellen*.

## BREAKING BARRIERS

DeGeneres shifted from comedian to historymaker when her character on *Ellen* came out as gay in 1997, becoming the first openly gay lead character on a sitcom. DeGeneres herself also came out at the same time. Although she and her show were applauded and supported for the groundbreaking decisions, they also faced a backlash. Some stations refused to air the episode, and sponsors began to withdraw advertisements. Despite winning an Emmy for the important episode, *Ellen* was canceled the following year. But DeGeneres had more to offer. She voiced the character of Dory in the film *Finding Nemo,* and she launched her own talk show in 2003: *The Ellen DeGeneres Show*. The show became a smash hit, receiving high ratings and multiple Emmy Awards. In 2008, when same-sex marriage became legal in California, DeGeneres married her partner, Portia de Rossi.

## GIVING BACK

Having already made history, DeGeneres continues to use her fame and platform to support others. On her talk show, DeGeneres often addresses pressing issues such as bullying and discrimination. Alongside de Rossi, DeGeneres also works as an animal rights advocate. In 2016, President Barack Obama awarded DeGeneres with the Presidential Medal of Freedom for her contribution to the arts. And as much as she is celebrated, DeGeneres continues to celebrate others and the differences that make them special.

**ELLEN DEGENERES** IS AN AMERICAN COMEDIAN AND TELEVISION HOST AND IS THE FIRST OPENLY GAY WOMAN TO HAVE HER OWN PRIME-TIME TELEVISION SHOW.

DeGeneres has hosted the GRAMMYS, the EMMYS, and the ACADEMY AWARDS!

# SCIENCE &

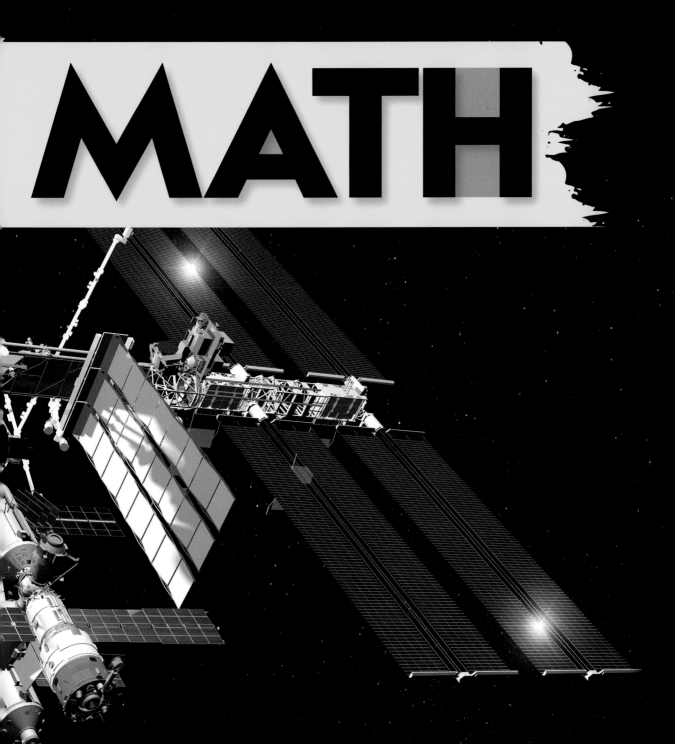

THE INTERNATIONAL SPACE STATION (ISS). IN 2020, NASA ASTRONAUT CHRISTINA KOCH RETURNED SAFELY TO EARTH AFTER SPENDING A RECORD-BREAKING 328 DAYS IN SPACE ON THE ISS. DURING THAT TIME, SHE WAS PART OF THE FIRST ALL-FEMALE SPACEWALK, SPENDING SEVEN HOURS OUTSIDE THE ISS WITH OTHER FEMALE ASTRONAUTS TO REPLACE A FAILED POWER CONTROL UNIT.

# MATH

# GiRLS CAN...
# DO MATH!

THE LACK OF WOMEN WORKING AND STUDYING IN MATHEMATICS AND SCIENCES PROBABLY COMES AS NO SURPRISE—AFTER ALL, IT IS A COMMON SUBJECT IN TODAY'S MEDIA. But where did this inequality in science, technology, engineering, and mathematics (STEM) come from? Plenty of research has shown that women are not only good at STEM subjects but also want to study them. So how did the myth that women aren't good at these things ever come about?

## SCHOOL'S OUT

Because women throughout history have been expected to tend to their homes, many cultures and societies saw no value in educating girls. In fact, many schools refused to admit girls at all. Although modern universities and colleges began appearing in the Middle Ages, women were largely not allowed to attend. Some wealthy women had access to tutors, but it took until the 1800s for colleges to start admitting female students. Even then, it was unusual, and far more so for women of color. In the United States, the ratio between men and women in higher education did not become equal until around 1970. The fact that only men had been able to go to college encouraged the incorrect belief that men were naturally smarter and that women did not belong in academics.

## DECODING DISCRIMINATION

Even after women had access to further education, the false notion that men were better at science and math was still a commonly held belief. This made it harder for women to be taken seriously in STEM subjects and

**MYTH #1:** MEN ARE **NATURALLY BETTER** AT SCIENCE AND MATH DUE TO BIOLOGICAL DIFFERENCES.

**FALSE!** Although this has been a popular theory for centuries, modern research shows that there is absolutely no connection between men and women's biological differences and their natural abilities in math or science. In fact, studies show that there is no natural gender difference in ability in these areas; most differences in mathematical or scientific abilities can largely be attributed to the fact that boys are more often encouraged to pursue STEM subjects than girls.

created biases that still exist today. In one field study, scientists created fictional graduate students of varying genders and race and sent meeting requests to faculty members. The results showed that faculty in STEM fields were much more likely to respond to white male candidates than to women or people of color. Research also showed that even with identical applications, faculty members rated male candidates higher. This widespread discrimination has made it difficult for women to earn math and science degrees and get jobs in these fields. Unfortunately, centuries of exclusion have led to many myths that women aren't as capable at STEM subjects as men. Take a look around this page at some of the stereotypes people have believed when it comes to women's abilities in math and science.

## RECOGNITION

Today, there is still much to overcome. Statistics from the Department of Labor show that in the United States, women hold only 25 percent of computer and mathematical jobs and account for only 20 percent of college students enrolled in computer science and engineering majors. The numbers also show that men in science and math jobs tend to make about $36.34 an hour, compared to the $31.11 an

**MYTH #2:** BOYS ARE NATURALLY **MORE INTERESTED** IN SCIENCE AND MATH.

**FALSE!** Studies show that boys are encouraged much more than girls are to study science and math, which results in more boys and men entering these fields. Some studies show that this type of biased encouragement starts as early as kindergarten.

hour women earn in the same fields. But today more women are earning STEM degrees than ever before, and the list of fantastic achievements by female scientists keeps growing. Plus, more and more people are recognizing and honoring the incredible women in history whose contributions had previously gone unnoticed. Take a look at some of the amazing women who prove that girls can excel at science and math!

**MYTH #3:** THE FACT THAT THERE AREN'T A LOT OF FAMOUS FEMALE SCIENTISTS OR MATHEMATICIANS PROVES THAT WOMEN **AREN'T AS GOOD** AT THOSE THINGS.

**FALSE!** Women have not had the same access or opportunities as men, but that does not mean they are not as naturally talented. There are tons of incredible female scientists and mathematicians—and there always have been! But these women tend to go unrecognized for their work, largely because of historical gender biases.

**MADAM C. J. WALKER** WAS THE INVENTOR OF THE REVOLUTIONARY HAIR-CARE REMEDY CALLED THE WALKER METHOD AND ONE OF THE FIRST BLACK FEMALE MILLIONAIRES IN THE UNITED STATES.

Walker opened the **LELIA COLLEGE OF BEAUTY CULTURE** in Pittsburgh, Pennsylvania, U.S.A., named for her daughter.

# INVENT PRO

BEST YET! FOR ALL THE FAMILY!

**MADAM WALKER'S** ALL-PURPOSE **HAIR CONDITIONING CREAM**

"FOR PERFECT DRESSING AND GROOMING"

## EARLY LIFE

Madam C. J. Walker (December 23, 1867–May 25, 1919) was born Sarah Breedlove on a cotton plantation near Delta, Louisiana, U.S.A. Though slavery was abolished before she was born, Walker faced a difficult life in a country filled with racism and coming to terms with the end of the Civil War. Orphaned at age seven, Walker was forced to work as a maid instead of going to school. She married at just 14 and was a widow and mother by the age of 20. She had few options, but Walker was determined to take care of her daughter. The two moved to St. Louis, Missouri, U.S.A., where Walker worked as an underpaid washerwoman.

## BECOMING MADAM C. J. WALKER

In addition to trying to support her family, Walker struggled to maintain a healthy head of hair at a time with no indoor plumbing. When a scalp infection caused her to lose most of her hair, she decided to find a cure. She experimented with different home remedies and store-bought options and found one that seemed to work: Wonderful Hair Grower. In 1905, Walker moved to Denver, Colorado, U.S.A., to work for its creator, Annie Turnbo Malone. Next, Walker took a job working for a pharmacist, which allowed her

to study chemistry. This new knowledge led to the solution she had been looking for: her own ointment that cured dandruff and other scalp ailments! She called it the Walker Method.

In addition to noticing a pattern of baldness in communities that lacked indoor plumbing, Walker identified two other problems: Black people were often banned from shopping in stores that sold beauty products, and black women had trouble finding jobs. She decided to build a company that could address all of these issues. Walker began selling the Walker Method door-to-door, and she soon hired other women to sell her products. In addition to addressing some of the challenges she saw in her community, Walker was one of the first black women to own her own business and soon became one of the first black female millionaires in the United States. Madam C. J. Walker grew into a well-known philanthropist who contributed time and money to charities and organizations that helped advance black people in the United States. She often spoke out publicly against violence against black people. Her legacy continues today: The Walker Method still serves as the foundation for many modern hair-care treatments.

## SOLVE PROBLEMS LIKE WALKER!

### THINK ABOUT SOLUTIONS

Walker saw a basic but universal problem in her community and set out to fix it. If you come across problems in your everyday life or hear about others struggling, this might be a great opportunity to create a solution.

### KNOW WHAT YOU DON'T KNOW

Realizing she didn't have all of the information she needed, Walker sought out jobs that provided the knowledge she wanted. No one starts out knowing everything! Seek out mentors or take classes in the areas related to the problems you are trying to solve.

# DUCTS

# BLAST
## OFF!

### PRE-ORBIT

Valentina Tereshkova (b. March 6, 1937) grew up in a small village called Maslennikovo in the Soviet Union (now Russia). At age 16, she had to leave school to work in a textile factory to earn money for her family. But Tereshkova didn't want to give up her education, so she took correspondence courses and communicated with teachers by mail. For fun, she enjoyed the unusual hobby of parachuting, joining the Yaroslavl Air Sports Club and completing more than 126 parachute jumps. When Yuri Gagarin became the first human to go to space in 1961, he inspired Tereshkova to go even further. Though she had no formal training, she wanted to see the universe beyond Earth's atmosphere.

### WHERE NO WOMAN HAD GONE BEFORE

The Soviet Union was seeking to put together a team of female cosmonauts, and more than 400 women applied for the job, including Tereshkova. She had no flight experience, but her parachute jumps set her apart and secured her a spot alongside four other finalists. Together, the women trained rigorously for a year and a half. In the end, only Tereshkova was nominated to travel into space on the Vostok 6 mission.

On the morning of June 16, 1963, Tereshkova entered the tiny Vostok 6 capsule and launched into orbit, becoming the first woman in space. For 71 hours, she floated along in Earth's orbit, keeping an informational log and taking photos for researchers. It was a successful mission, despite an error in the capsule's navigating software. When Tereshkova noticed the Vostok 6 was moving away from Earth, she contacted Mission Control. Scientists quickly fixed the problem, and she landed safely. Tereshkova returned a hero, celebrated and honored for her service.

Though she received many awards and went on to a successful political career, 19 years went by before the program sent another woman into space, cosmonaut Svetlana Savitskaya. One year after that, Sally Ride became the first American woman in space, though she faced so much sexism that she nearly didn't earn that achievement. When journalists questioned whether Ride's body could withstand the dangers of space, Tereshkova stepped in to defend her. Today, Tereshkova continues to be a role model and champion of women, having blazed a path to the stars that 59 other women have since followed.

BEFORE A MAN WALKED ON THE MOON, A WOMAN ORBITED EARTH. **VALENTINA TERESHKOVA,** A RETIRED RUSSIAN COSMONAUT, WAS THE FIRST WOMAN TO GO TO SPACE.

Tereshkova has **CARRIED THE OLYMPIC TORCH** twice—in 2008 and 2014.

# TEACH OTHERS

## A SURPRISING SCHOLAR

A typical search for great philosophers and mathematicians might not turn up any women at all. But Hypatia deserves the same name recognition enjoyed by Plato, Confucius, and Einstein.

Hypatia (circa 350–415 C.E.) was born in Alexandria, Egypt, and grew up studying academics. Her father, Theon, was a professor at the famous University of Alexandria. Though women at the time were expected to lead domestic lives, Theon tutored his daughter in the sciences. None of Hypatia's works are thought to survive (although some historians believe that Hypatia actually wrote one of Theon's works). However, writings by Hypatia's peers show that she was gifted in math, philosophy of the natural world, and astronomy. In fact, Hypatia was so well known for her intellect that she ran her own school, where she taught students how to construct astronomical equipment. She was famous for her popular public lectures, which drew crowds that gathered to listen to her. Unfortunately, despite Hypatia's brilliance—and sometimes, because of it—she had dangerous enemies as well.

## REMEMBERED BY HISTORY

At the height of Hypatia's career, Alexandria was an unstable place. Many academic subjects that had previously been popular were now considered heretical in the eyes of the new bishop, Cyril. Cyril had ordered the destruction of many existing temples and statues because he favored the new religion, Christianity. He also targeted some intellectuals. Hypatia was an obvious target as a female scholar, and she stood out even among her peers. She had refused to marry, often wore men's scholarly robes, practiced a pagan religion, and had made friends with some of Cyril's enemies. While in the city one day, a mob of monks attacked and killed her. After her death, Cyril went on to destroy the University of Alexandria and exile many other scholars. Even though they intended to strike Hypatia's name from history forever, their actions had the opposite effect: Hypatia's extraordinary life and untimely death solidified her place in history. In the centuries that followed, her story continued to be told, and she remains a symbol of strength for female scholars everywhere.

**HYPATIA OF ALEXANDRIA** WAS AN ANCIENT EGYPTIAN PHILOSOPHER, MATHEMATICIAN, AND ASTRONOMER. SHE IS CELEBRATED AS A BRILLIANT LEADER AND TEACHER.

"HYPATIA" comes from the Greek word for "supreme."

## A MATHEMATICAL MARVEL

In NASA's earliest days, the people who designed, built, and programmed rocket computers were mostly male and usually white. Katherine Johnson (August 26, 1918–February 24, 2020), born in West Virginia, U.S.A., was neither, and she came of age during a time when discriminatory laws prevented black students from attending schools with their white peers. Johnson was brilliant—she started high school at 13 years old and by 18, she was blasting through her college's rigorous mathematics program. She graduated at just 19.

## THE SPACE RACE

Though she attended a prestigious graduate school, Johnson soon left the program to raise her family. But when she learned about a position at the National Advisory Committee for Aeronautics (NACA), Johnson and her husband moved their family so that she could pursue it. In 1953, Johnson

**KATHERINE JOHNSON** WAS A MATHEMATICIAN WHO DIRECTLY INFLUENCED AMERICAN SPACE TRAVEL.

# SHOOT FOR THE

was hired by NACA to work with the segregated West Area Computing unit. This skillful group of black women assisted engineers by completing long mathematical calculations by hand. They were known as Computers, and the success of the early U.S. space program depended on them. Despite their hard work, these women still faced segregation each day and were forced to use separate bathrooms and dining facilities. The policy of segregation finally ended in 1958, when NACA became the brand-new National Aeronautics and Space Administration—also known as NASA.

NASA's goal was to make the United States the first country to send a person into space. Johnson was promoted to the Space Task Group, and she and an engineer from the group wrote a report that predicted calculations needed to send a spacecraft into orbit. Johnson became the first woman in the entire division to be credited as the author of a research report.

## A CRUCIAL CALCULATION

In 1962, NASA was preparing for the Friendship 7 mission, which would send astronaut John Glenn around Earth. The complex mission depended on a network of computers, but they were notorious for breaking down, and if anything went wrong, the mission would be a one-way trip. Before blastoff, Glenn specifically requested that Johnson approve the computers' calculations. He agreed to fly only if she gave the all clear. The catch was that Johnson had to recalculate everything by hand. She did—and the mission was a success, with Glenn orbiting Earth for 4 hours and 53 minutes.

Johnson's contributions to NASA and the U.S. space race were singular, and over the years she received numerous awards and honors for her work, including the Presidential Medal of Freedom. Her genius not only contributed to science research, but also changed the very course of history.

JOHNSON SOLVING EQUATIONS AT NASA

## SOLVE PROBLEMS LIKE JOHNSON!

### TAKE ADVANTAGE OF OPPORTUNITIES

Johnson was born in an era of segregation and faced many unfair rules and policies. But when she encountered an opportunity, such as working for NASA, she pursued it fully and even moved to another city. If you come across the chance to follow your passions, seize it!

### KEEP WORKING

Though her important contributions went mostly unrecognized for a long time, Johnson was proud of what she did and continued to work hard. Keep going even when times are tough; persistence will help you achieve your goals.

### DO WHAT YOU LOVE

Johnson once said, "I loved going to work every single day." Find something that you are passionate about—the more excited you are to dive into work, the more of an impact you might have!

The movie *HIDDEN FIGURES* is based on the lives of Johnson and other black female mathematicians.

# STARS

# INVENTIONS BY WOMEN

## WHO IS THE **MOST FAMOUS SCIENTIST** YOU KNOW?

When most people think of inventors, they may picture men—maybe mad scientists in laboratories or young computer geniuses developing new programs and codes. This is largely due to the biases that society has around science, math, and engineering and what is often presented in movies and TV shows. But the truth is that women also tinker, create, and innovate. In fact, women have invented tons of remarkable technologies that we use every day! Check out these amazing inventions made by women.

## SOLVE PROBLEMS!

**Have an urge to invent?** Get started at home! Many inventions (such as Parker's central heating furnace mentioned at right) have been dreamed up in people's homes or garages. Ask an adult if you can carve out a space to tinker and get experimenting. (But remember: Always have an adult on hand if you're using any dangerous tools or ingredients.)

## SPACE STATION BATTERIES

It might seem crazy, but the International Space Station (ISS) is powered partially by batteries! And these batteries, which can be recharged tens of thousands of times, were invented by a woman: Olga González-Sanabria. González-Sanabria is from Puerto Rico and joined NASA in 1979. In 1998, her batteries were launched into space alongside a fuel storage unit as the first pieces of the ISS. With the aid of solar panels, they powered the ISS until 2017, when they were replaced with newer versions.

## SECRET WARTIME COMMUNICATIONS

Hedy Lamarr, born in Austria as Hedwig Eva Maria Kiesler, was a glamorous film star of the 1930s and '40s. Everyone praised her looks, but no one thought much about her brain. But Lamarr was brilliant. During World War II, she devised a secret wartime communication, known as frequency hopping, that allowed people to communicate over the radio without having their signals jammed by enemies. Though the system was never used during the war, the Navy began to experiment with the invention in the 1950s; Lamarr's frequency hopping ultimately helped lay the foundation for the inventions of Wi-Fi, Bluetooth, and GPS!

## MODERN COMPUTERS

There's no clear answer as to who invented the computer. Many people think of Bill Gates and Steve Jobs, while most scientists credit Charles Babbage (who developed an automatic calculator around 1812). Some historians point to a newly discovered ancient Greek machine called the Antikythera. But the truth is that the modern computers we know today wouldn't exist without Ada Lovelace or Grace Hopper. Lovelace, who worked with Babbage on his designs, is often known as the "first programmer" for her instructions about how to create codes that would allow the machine to process letters and symbols. A little more than a century later, Navy admiral Grace Hopper invented the first compiler, a program that allowed computers to "understand" English-language instructions. Thanks to their efforts, modern computers can both "think" and process language, numbers, and symbols.

## CENTRAL HEATING

Think of all the winter nights you've spent cozy and warm at home. You have Alice H. Parker to thank for that! While it's possible to heat homes using wood and coal in open fires and fireplaces, Parker believed she could come up with a safer, more reliable way. In 1919, she patented a central heating furnace that relied on natural gas. Her system was not only much safer, it was also more energy efficient and able to heat entire buildings. Parker's invention led the way to what we now know as central heating.

**FE VILLANUEVA DEL MUNDO** WAS A HISTORY-MAKING DOCTOR CREDITED WITH BRINGING MEDICAL CARE FOR CHILDREN AND BABIES TO THE PHILIPPINES.

Del Mundo was awarded the title of **NATIONAL SCIENTIST OF THE PHILIPPINES.**

# SAVE LIVES

## A BETTER FUTURE

Born in Manila, Philippines, Fe Villanueva del Mundo (November 27, 1911–August 6, 2011) was one of eight children. Unfortunately, three of her siblings died as infants. Because of their deaths, del Mundo's sister Elisa dreamed of becoming a doctor. But when she came down with an abdominal infection and passed away, del Mundo decided she would take up medicine and save lives in her sister's honor.

## A BRILLIANT STUDENT

Del Mundo began her college studies at just 15 and graduated at the top of her class in 1933. As a student, she interned in her home province of Marinduque and learned that the tragic losses her family had faced were quite common. Many children received no medical care, and no available doctors specialized in children's health care (known as pediatrics). So when President Manuel Quezon noticed del Mundo's accomplishments and offered to sponsor her at any medical program in the United States, she chose to study pediatrics at Harvard.

Del Mundo arrived at Harvard Medical School in 1936, only to find that the school did not yet admit female students. Officials had accepted del Mundo without realizing she was a woman! Due to her exceptional knowledge and skill, the school allowed her to stay, making del Mundo the first female student to attend Harvard. She excelled and went on to study at many other prestigious universities.

## SAVING LIVES

By 1941, del Mundo was ready to return home. Her help was greatly needed there, as World War II had begun and Japan invaded the Philippines on December 8, 1941, leaving many people injured and displaced. Del Mundo quickly joined the International Red Cross and set up a makeshift camp called the Children's Home to care for children affected by the war. She became known as the "Angel of Santo Tomas." The Children's Home was shut down in 1943, and del Mundo resolved to find a way to continue serving the children of the Philippines.

She became the director of Manila's North General Hospital, which allowed her to broaden her impact. But she still dreamed of running a hospital dedicated to pediatrics. After the war, del Mundo sold her home and most of her possessions and took out a loan to open the Children's Medical Center in 1957 in Quezon City. It was the first pediatric hospital in the Philippines. Del Mundo's influence grew as she trained doctors, nurses, and paramedics to serve rural areas.

By the time del Mundo passed away in 2011, she had gained international acclaim, published more than 100 medical articles, and invented an incubator that could be used in rural areas with no electricity. But her biggest achievement was the impact she had on thousands of children and medical professionals who benefited from her work.

# SOLVE PROBLEMS LIKE DEL MUNDO!

### GROW FROM YOUR EXPERIENCES

Del Mundo lost four of her siblings during childhood, including her beloved sister Elisa. Del Mundo took up medicine in Elisa's honor and ended up saving countless children in her country. Remember that you have the power to fight against the things that might be affecting those you love and to make the world better for others.

### BE WILLING TO SACRIFICE

To open her own medical center, del Mundo sold her home and most of her things. If you have a goal you want to accomplish, a school you want to attend, a product you want to invent, or something else, consider what you are willing to do to get there, whether giving up your weekends to study, using an allowance to buy materials, or something else.

# FIX PROB

**GITANJALI RAO** IS A YOUNG SCIENTIST AND INVENTOR WHO CREATED AN INNOVATIVE METHOD OF TESTING FOR LEAD IN WATER AS A RESPONSE TO THE FLINT WATER CRISIS.

Rao likes to name all of her inventions after **MYTHOLOGICAL CHARACTERS.**

## FLINT WATER CRISIS

In 2014, a crisis hit the city of Flint, Michigan, U.S.A., when city officials decided to change their water source to the Flint River. Flint, an impoverished city with a largely black population, had long been neglected, and its water had suffered from pollution before. Unfortunately, things got much worse with the new water source. Officials failed to properly treat the water from the Flint River, and though they claimed it was safe to drink, the pollution in it began to wear away the city's old pipes, causing lead to seep into the drinking supply. The water for the people of Flint was dangerously contaminated. Lead can cause developmental problems in children, behavioral changes, and damage to people's brains, kidneys, and livers. Exposure to too much lead can even cause death. The drinking water in Flint was found to contain lead levels twelve to hundreds of times higher than what is considered safe, and up to 12,000 children had been exposed. Officials eventually switched the drinking source back to Lake Huron, but a 2016 study showed high levels of lead remained in the water. Even though efforts were being made to restore Flint's safe

# LEMS

RAO DEMONSTRATING TETHYS

water supply, the technology needed to detect lead in water wasn't good enough to prevent this type of disaster from happening again.

## STEPPING UP

Many adult scientists and activists responded to the crisis in Flint, but one of the biggest breakthroughs in new technology came from then 12-year-old Gitanjali Rao (b. 2005). Rao was born in Lone Tree, Colorado, U.S.A., and grew up with parents who encouraged her to experiment and invent. She first learned about the Flint water crisis from the news and noticed her parents attempting to test for lead in their own water. Rao realized that the current methods made it difficult to get accurate results. She wanted to fix that, so she got to work.

During her research, Rao came across nanotechnology, an area of science that includes building machines at teeny-tiny subatomic and molecular scales to create new materials and medicines and make superfast computer chips. Rao learned about a device that used nanotechnology to detect harmful gases—could she create one to detect lead?

## TINY TECHNOLOGY, HUGE IMPACT

Rao began experimenting and invented a tool that, when dipped into water, could react to any lead present and send an alert to a phone app, which Rao also developed. She named the tool Tethys, after the Greek goddess of fresh water. Rao submitted Tethys to the Discovery Education and 3M Young Scientist Challenge and won.

Rao earned $25,000 with her win, and she went on to receive an additional $25,000 from the 2018 MAKERS conference. She plans to use the money to further develop Tethys and make it available across the world. In 2018, Rao presented a TEDx Talk and received the United States Environmental Protection Agency's President's Environmental Youth Award. Rao has used her platform to speak out against the pay gap between men and women. As one of the youngest scientists in the world, she is leading the charge for safer water—and for women in science.

# SOLVE PROBLEMS LIKE RAO!

## SET UP A LAB

With the help of her parents, Rao experimented around the house and in her yard. Ask an adult to help you create a space where you can tinker and invent to your heart's content. But remember to be safe—Rao recommends reaching out to local research facilities or chemistry labs if you plan to work with any potentially dangerous materials.

## SUBMIT YOUR IDEAS

After Rao submitted Tethys as part of a challenge for young scientists, she won money to continue developing her tool, plus the chance to speak with experts and present her ideas to others. Investigate local and international competitions and challenges where you can submit your ideas or inventions. Even if you don't win, you're sure to meet experts, mentors, and friends!

RAO ON *THE TONIGHT SHOW* WITH JIMMY FALLON

# JENNIFER DOUDNA

In 2012, Jennifer Doudna and her research partner made one of the most significant discoveries in the history of biochemistry—how an enzyme called Cas9 could be combined with a molecular sequence called CRISPR to cut DNA strands with precision. The result was a revolutionary new gene-editing technique. Today, Doudna is a professor at the University of California, Berkeley, and advocates for applying ethical standards to scientific advances.

## WHAT DO YOU THINK IS THE SINGLE MOST IMPORTANT CHANGE THAT NEEDS TO HAPPEN FOR WOMEN IN THE NEXT 10 YEARS?

 **DOUDNA:** It really comes down to women feeling that they are welcome in all sectors of professional life—that includes in business, in board rooms, and in leadership roles in companies, as well as in academia, which is, of course, my line of work.

## WHAT IS YOUR MOST CONSPICUOUS CHARACTER TRAIT?

 **DOUDNA:** My dedication. I do feel very much that I'm deeply dedicated to what I'm doing in my life, whether it's in my professional life with the people I work with, or in my homelife with my husband and child. I feel very committed to the decisions that I've made about who I am and what I'm doing right now in my life, and that I want to follow through on my commitments.

## WHAT ADVICE WOULD YOU GIVE YOUNG WOMEN TODAY?

 **DOUDNA:** I encourage women to take charge and try to project self-confidence even if they don't feel it because sometimes you need to do that.

## WHAT DO YOU THINK IS THE MOST IMPORTANT CHALLENGE FACING WOMEN TODAY?

 **DOUDNA:** I think in general women tend to doubt their abilities much more than men do. When I speak with my female students, friends, and colleagues about these issues, I tell them to find mentors, whether they are female or male, who will support them and help them reach their full potential, so they will develop the confidence to meet life's challenges, whatever they are.

# ASHA DE VOS

Asha de Vos is a marine biologist and conservationist from Sri Lanka who specializes in researching and working with marine mammals. She is the founder of Oceanswell, Sri Lanka's first marine conservation research and education organization, and also oversees the Sri Lankan Blue Whale Project, the first endeavor to focus on a unique population of blue whales in the northern Indian Ocean. In addition to that, she acts as an ocean educator and mentors more than 30 students from underrepresented nations in marine conservation each year.

## WHAT DO YOU THINK IS THE MOST IMPORTANT CHALLENGE FACING WOMEN TODAY?

 **DE VOS:** Sometimes where I come from, Sri Lanka, there's almost amazement when women achieve things. With my work, for example, most people say things like, "But you're doing a man's job, right?" They're not considering the fact that it doesn't matter who you are or what your gender is. If there's a job to be done, anybody can and should be able to do it. At some point we will value women and diversity and the fact that you don't have to be a man to do some of the stuff that we do. But at the moment we're still struggling with trying to bring everyone up to speed and create that equality.

## WHAT DO YOU THINK IS THE SINGLE MOST IMPORTANT CHANGE THAT NEEDS TO HAPPEN FOR WOMEN IN THE NEXT 10 YEARS?

 **DE VOS:** I think there has to be more role modeling of women— for men and for women, for boys and for girls. The achievements of women have to be showcased with as much excitement as those of men, and not just to women. Women shouldn't just be role models for only women and girls; women should be seen as role models to boys as well. That can change things for future generations.

## WHAT WERE THE BIGGEST HURDLES THAT YOU HAD TO OVERCOME?

**DE VOS:** Marine conservation was pretty unheard of in Sri Lanka before I started. When I told people I wanted to be a marine biologist, I did get a lot of backlash. I had to prove myself and work harder to make sure that I could just keep plowing through for this goal of mine.

Globally, the other challenge was I come from a small tropical island, and marine conservation is very, very Western-centric. When I started talking about my work, there were lots of people who wanted to come and take over because they didn't believe that we had the capacity. So I had to prove not just that I am capable as a woman, but that my country is completely capable.

**SARA JOSEPHINE BAKER** WAS A PIONEER IN MEDICINE AND PUBLIC HEALTH WHOSE WORK DRAMATICALLY REDUCED THE DEATH RATES OF INFANTS AND CHILDREN IN NEW YORK CITY. HER EFFORTS REMAIN THE FOUNDATION FOR MANY POLICIES IN PUBLIC HEALTH TODAY.

## A RISKY CHOICE

Sara Josephine Baker (November 15, 1873–February 22, 1945) was born in Poughkeepsie, New York, U.S.A. As she was planning to leave for Vassar—then a women's college— her father and brother suddenly succumbed to typhoid fever, one of many devastating diseases in the late 1800s. Baker was only 16 but suddenly faced the responsibility of providing for her family. She decided to study medicine, which was considered a secure profession, even though few medical schools were open to women and less than 1 percent of physicians were female. It was a risky choice, but Baker was determined to succeed.

## CHOOSING MEDICINE

Baker did well and earned an internship in Boston, Massachusetts, U.S.A., where she noticed a clear connection between poverty and illness. She felt a duty to commit herself to social medicine—the practice of creating healthier conditions for

# REDEFINE HEALTH

those living in poverty. After graduating, Baker went to New York City, where conditions were even worse than in Boston. With hundreds of people crammed into crumbling apartment buildings known as slums, sickness and disease spread quickly. Contagious illnesses were so commonplace that it was hard for children to survive to even five years old. Determined to help, Baker became an inspector for the New York City Department of Health, and by 1907 she was the assistant to the commissioner of health. She developed new approaches to infectious disease and preventive health care plans for children.

Baker focused on teaching healthy hygiene practices to people forced to live in slums, and she created "baby health stations," where clean milk was distributed. She also established programs to teach mothers and other caretakers about proper infant care. Baker's approach had a major economic impact because mothers could go to work knowing their babies were safely with other caretakers. She also introduced proper storage for medicines, which reduced infant blindness, and campaigned for the state to regulate midwives. All of

BAKER IN
NEW YORK CITY

Baker's efforts led to a drastic drop in infant mortality.

Next, she turned her attention to older children, who were often malnourished and sick. She created a school health program, which introduced school nurses and school lunches. Baker began to be recognized for her work, and as her fame grew, so did the impact of her efforts. Many government programs were created based on her findings, and the country began to prioritize health and wellness of infants and children for the first time. Her contributions remain the foundation of child health care.

## SOLVE PROBLEMS LIKE BAKER!

### LEND A HAND TO THOSE IN NEED
Baker started out with a personal goal to help her family but quickly saw that she could make an impact on many more people. If you see a friend—or anyone—struggling, see how you can lend a hand.

### CAUSE A CHAIN REACTION
It's hard to imagine that one person's ideas can have the kind of worldwide impact that Baker's did, but they can. Helping to solve a problem in your community could end up helping others around the globe. No problem is too small to solve!

### TAKE RISKS
Almost no women were physicians, but Baker pursued her chosen career anyway. Taking risks can be scary—and they don't always work out!—but it is an important step for change.

# CARE +

# DISCOVER
## NEW SPECIES

**ISABELLA AIONA ABBOTT** WAS A LEADING BIOLOGIST AND THE FIRST EVER NATIVE HAWAIIAN WOMAN TO EARN A PH.D. IN SCIENCE.

Many **DIFFERENT SPECIES OF ALGAE** have been named after Abbott.

## EARLY SEEDS

Dr. Isabella Kauakea Yau Yung Aiona Abbott (June 20, 1919–October 28, 2010) spent her childhood exploring the beaches of her native Maui, Hawaii, U.S.A. There she developed her interest in algae—or *limu,* as it is called in Hawaiian. She and her family often gathered limu to be used in traditional Hawaiian meals, and her mother knew the Hawaiian name for every kind of algae and whether it was edible. Abbott's fascination with algae eventually led her to study biology.

## IN BLOOM

Abbott earned several degrees in botany before pursuing her Ph.D. at the University of California, Berkeley, in 1950. There, she met and married Don Abbott, all while on her way to becoming the first Native Hawaiian woman to earn a Ph.D. in science. The pair then moved to Pacific Grove, California, U.S.A., for Don's job at Stanford University's Hopkins Marine Station. Unfortunately for Abbott, finding work was not so easy. In an era when women in general were shut out of scientific jobs, and when Native Hawaiians struggled for independence, Abbott faced almost impossible obstacles as a woman of color despite her knowledge and impressive education. She chose instead to focus on raising her daughter, Annie, and continued to study limu on her own.

Abbott never lost sight of her dream, and in 1960, 10 years after receiving her Ph.D., she was hired as a lecturer at Hopkins. Though algae may not look like much, Abbott's work proved just how important they are—it turns out the marine organisms provide more than 75 percent of Earth's oxygen! Abbott went on to become the first female faculty member of Stanford University's biological sciences department, and in 1972, she became the department's first female professor and first professor of color. During her career, she received many awards and prizes and is credited with discovering more than two hundred different algae species. Abbott retired in 1982 and passed away in 2010, but her lifelong studies remain the definitive guide to some of the most important organisms on the planet: limu. Her contributions have inspired generations of women and people of color to dedicate themselves to science.

# MAKE WAVES

KATIJA AND FELLOW RESEARCHERS TAGGING JELLYFISH

## BORN A SCIENTIST

Kakani Katija (b. August 14, 1982) grew up wanting to be an astronaut. Little did she know that she'd actually one day search for alien life—just not in space! Katija's parents supported her dreams of becoming a scientist, and she received a degree in aeronautics and astronautics, as well as a master's degree in aeronautics. However, Katija found that her attention had begun to drift away from space and toward a place also not fully explored but closer to home—the ocean.

## UNDERWATER ALIENS

Only 95 percent of the ocean has been explored, and less than 1 percent of the ocean floor has been mapped. But unlike space, the ocean is full of life. Katija became interested in studying the way marine life moves and in developing new ways to explore and understand this vast, uncharted area. During a project studying jellyfish, Katija used lasers and dye to track their movements. What she found was surprising: It turns out jellyfish not only pull water into their bells (their umbrella-shaped bodies), they also drag streams of water behind them as they move. This simple discovery has huge implications—jellyfish might actually contribute to the mixing of the ocean and to its currents, which could be important information for helping to preserve the ocean and its ecosystems as climate change worsens.

Katija also decided to investigate new, less invasive ways of exploring the ocean. She began by helping to invent a small new tool called the DeepPIV. So compact it can be carried by one scuba diver, the DeepPIV uses lasers to help track the movements of tiny marine invertebrate organisms called larvaceans. It can be attached to remotely operated vehicles (ROVs) to help track organisms at great depths. Katija is also working on developing an ROV called the Mesobot, which will allow scientists to monitor underwater organisms without causing any stress or interference. Another device, the ITAG, lets scientists safely tag larger organisms and track their movements and behavior. By inventing new tools for the scientific community, Katija hopes to expand the scope of ocean exploration!

**KAKANI KATIJA** IS A NATIONAL GEOGRAPHIC EXPLORER, A BIOLOGIST, AND AN ENGINEER WHO HELPS SEARCH FOR UNDISCOVERED UNDERWATER LIFE.

Many of the creatures Katija studies are **NOCTURNAL,** which means she doesn't get much sleep when she's doing research.

# WIN THE

## MARIE CURIE
WAS A BRILLIANT PHYSICIST WHOSE GROUNDBREAKING WORK IN RADIATION LED HER TO BECOME THE FIRST WOMAN TO RECEIVE A NOBEL PRIZE.

One of Curie's daughters **ALSO WON THE NOBEL PRIZE** in Chemistry.

## A SUPPORTIVE FAMILY

Born Maria Sklodowska, Marie Curie (November 7, 1867–July 4, 1934) was from Warsaw Poland. Her parents, both teachers were determined to give their children good educations. Life was difficult for young Curie; at the time, the area of modern-day Poland was under the Russian Empire, and tensions were high. Curie's father lost his job, and when Curie was 10, her oldest sister, Zofia, contracted typhus and died. Unfortunately, Curie's mother died from tuberculosis only two years later. The family's misfortunes made it nearly impossible to afford school, but Curie and her sister Bronislawa made a pact: Curie would work to help pay for Bronislawa's education, and when Bronislawa graduated, she would help pay for Curie's education. University education was uncommon for women at the time, so the sisters set their sights on one university that did enroll women: the Sorbonne in Paris, France.

## BREAKTHROUGH DISCOVERIES

Bronislawa graduated and became a doctor thanks to Curie funding her education. While she worked to support her sister, Curie had read as

# NOBEL PRIZE

much as possible, and when it was her turn to go to the Sorbonne, she earned her physics degree in only three years. During that time Curie met and fell in love with fellow scientist Pierre Curie. They married in 1895 and began to work together on scientific experiments. They focused on studying uranium because Curie was intrigued by a recent discovery another scientist, Antoine Henri Becquerel, had made. The Curies' history-making research led them to discover radioactivity, which eventually led to modern forms of cancer treatment.

They also discovered two new elements—Curie named one new element polonium after her beloved Poland and the other radium due to the strong rays it produced. In 1903, Curie, Pierre, and Henri Becquerel all received the Nobel Prize in Physics for their work in radiation, making Curie the first woman ever to be awarded a Nobel Prize.

## DEVOTED TO SCIENCE

Unfortunately, in 1906, disaster struck when Pierre was killed by a horse carriage. But Curie continued to devote her life to science, stepping into Pierre's job as professor of physics at the Sorbonne. She was the first woman to teach at the university. In 1911, she won a second Nobel Prize in Chemistry for her discovery of polonium and radium, becoming the first person—male or female—to receive two Nobel Prizes.

Unfortunately, on July 4, 1934, after a lifetime of dedicated work, Curie died from overexposure to radiation. Her work inspired generations of women and scientists, and her research led to safety regulations to protect scientists from overexposure. The Curie Institute, a cancer research facility Curie founded in 1921, is still breaking scientific ground today.

CURIE IN HER LAB

## SOLVE PROBLEMS LIKE CURIE!

### IT'S NEVER TOO LATE FOR AN EDUCATION

Curie and her sister promised each other they would both receive their educations. Curie waited patiently until her sister had finished, and then went back to school herself. Even if you can't take certain classes or go to college right away, you can always go back to school—at any age!

# CHANG
# WORLD

# ING THE

# GIRLS CAN ...
# CHANGE THE WORLD!

WOMEN HAVE BEEN CHANGING THE WORLD SINCE BEFORE RECORDED HISTORY. As you've seen in this book, they have led nations, made scientific discoveries, broken records, created timeless works of art, and redefined their own femininity. They have also overcome discrimination, sexism, and oppressive laws. Many people—men and women—celebrate these icons for their achievements and support the women today who continue to strengthen communities, organize movements, and better the world. But some people still incorrectly believe that women can't make a difference—or that they shouldn't try. Take a look at the myths on this page and see if there is any truth to the claims.

GIRLS CAN!

## MYTH #1: WOMEN HAVEN'T CHANGED HISTORY.

**FALSE!** By now, you know this one is obviously untrue. Women have been changing history from ancient times right up until today. But why are so many women overlooked by history? A lot of it has to do with long-standing bias against their gender and because many scholars and historians who recorded history were men telling their own stories. Just think of the word "history"—*his story.* In many cases, the historians were political opponents intentionally trying to make their female enemies sound bad. It's likely because of this that women like Cleopatra and Wu Zetian became known as seductresses and murderers. Others who lost their battles, like Zenobia and Boudicca, were largely ignored by the victors.

Women also have had their achievements go unmentioned because of the many biases against their gender. A recent investigation by National Public Radio found scores of women who contributed research, copyediting, translating, transcribing, editing, and more for the works of their husbands or fathers but never received credit for their efforts.

## MYTH #2: WOMEN'S RIGHTS ARE NOT A PRIORITY.

**FALSE!** Studies show that empowering women has a ripple effect that improves communities around the world. Research has found that when girls have access to education, populations see better economies and healthier children, as well as decreases in infant mortality, deaths during childbirth, and child marriages. Other studies have shown that countries with more women in government experience less corruption.

## MYTH #3: WOMEN ARE ALREADY EQUAL.

**FALSE!** Though some people claim that women have already achieved equality, evidence from around the world overwhelmingly contradicts this. According to the United Nations, despite the fact that 143 of 195 countries guarantee equal rights for women in their constitutions, discrimination still exists in laws and policies, stereotypes, and social practices. Many women are still denied basic rights such as property ownership and financial independence.

Even in the United States, which claims equality, women are more likely to live in poverty and are underrepresented in government, business, and academia. And although Congress passed an Equal Rights Amendment in 1972 that would guarantee the same rights to both sexes, it was never ratified—meaning it is not a part of the Constitution.

**NOT ONLY ARE WOMEN CHANGING THE WORLD,** but it's important for them to do so! Check out some of the amazing women who have changed the rules—and the world.

ACTIVIST **MALALA YOUSAFZAI** ADVOCATES FOR GIRLS' EDUCATION IN PAKISTAN, DESPITE A HORRIFYING ASSASSINATION ATTEMPT.

## A YOUNG STUDENT

When Malala Yousafzai was born in Mingora, Pakistan, on July 12, 1997, the country was not a welcoming place for girls. But her father was an educator and an activist, and he was determined to give Yousafzai the same opportunities a boy would have. He founded the Khushal Girls High School and encouraged Yousafzai's studies. Things took a steep turn for the worse in 2007, though, when a fundamentalist Muslim group called the Tehrik-e-Taliban (known as the Taliban) invaded their area. The Taliban began to enforce strict Islamic law on the people. Girls' schools were destroyed or shut down, and women were banned from active roles in society. But Yousafzai refused to give up her right to an education.

## FIGHTING BACK

At just 11 years old, Yousafzai joined a protest against the school closings and gave a speech entitled "How Dare the Taliban Take Away My Basic Right to Education?"

The speech became famous, making its way throughout all of

YOUSAFZAI RECEIVING THE NOBEL PEACE PRIZE

Pakistan. Yousafzai soon began writing a blog about daily life under the Taliban using the alias "Gul Makai." It was incredibly dangerous, but also incredibly important.

At the same time, Yousafzai began to make public appearances, and she spoke out against a ban on television in 2009. She worked on two short films to promote education for girls. Soon, people realized that the blogger "Gul Makai" was really Yousafzai. She received Pakistan's first National Youth Peace Prize (later renamed the National Malala Peace Prize), but the recognition put Yousafzai in grave danger.

## AN INCREDIBLE RECOVERY

On October 9, 2012, Yousafzai was traveling home from school when a Taliban gunman shot her in the head. Amazingly, she survived and was flown to Birmingham, England, for surgery. Protests and an outpouring of support erupted around the world as millions took up

# TAKE A STAND

Yousafzai's cause in her honor. The United Nations, a global peace organization, introduced a petition that called for children everywhere to be allowed to return to school. As a result, Pakistan signed its first Right to Education bill in 2012.

As Yousafzai recovered, she settled into life in England and began to attend school. She knew that if she kept speaking out, she would continue to be a target for the Taliban. But she decided she could not stay quiet because others were still being denied an education. In 2013, she founded the Malala Fund, a nonprofit organization dedicated to promoting girls' rights to education.

## EDUCATION FOR ALL

Yousafzai's work has inspired countless people. In 2013, she received the United Nations Human Rights Prize and was named one of *Time* magazine's most influential people. In 2014, she became the youngest recipient ever of the Nobel Peace Prize. Yousafzai has used her platform to open multiple girls' schools in areas where education is not readily accessible and has helped provide schooling for refugees. She aims to create a world where everyone—no matter their gender or situation—has access to learning.

YOUSAFZAI BEING HONORED AT THE UNITED NATIONS YOUTH ASSEMBLY

Yousafzai was named after an Afghani folk hero, **MALALAI OF MAIWAND.**

# GET THE VOTE

**SUSAN B. ANTHONY** WAS AN AMERICAN ACTIVIST BEST KNOWN FOR HER PIVOTAL ROLE IN THE FIGHT FOR WOMEN'S RIGHT TO VOTE.

Anthony was the first woman to have her **PORTRAIT PRINTED ON A U.S. DOLLAR COIN.**

ANTHONY FEATURED ON
THE U.S. DOLLAR COIN

## SPEAKING FOR HERSELF

Susan B. Anthony (February 15, 1820–March 13, 1906) was born in Adams, Massachusetts, U.S.A., to a Quaker family that was passionate about social change. The Quaker religion promotes peace and equal rights for everyone, and Anthony started advocating for these ideas early in life. She began by distributing pamphlets that protested the enslavement of black people. As she worked, she encountered more and more prejudice against women. She soon realized that women would never be taken seriously in politics and social movements until they had the right to vote. When Anthony met fellow abolitionist Elizabeth Cady Stanton at an antislavery conference in 1851, the two became close friends and took their advocacy to the next level.

Anthony and Stanton devoted themselves to women's suffrage—the right of women to vote—and bringing the issue into the national spotlight. They spent years speaking, traveling, and advocating tirelessly for women to have the right to vote and own property. Together they founded several organizations to promote their cause. In 1866, they also began a women's rights publication called *The Revolution*, and a year later established the National Woman Suffrage Association. Many

people—men and women—opposed the movement and spoke out against Anthony and Stanton, claiming that women were too emotional to participate in politics. Opponents also worried that if women could vote, they might decide not to stay at home and take care of their families. But Anthony and Stanton refused to be silenced. In 1872, Anthony even illegally voted in the presidential election!

## A VOICE FOR (SOME) WOMEN

By the early 1900s, more and more women were interested in gaining the right to vote and being involved in politics. But although Anthony's important fight made her a feminist, it did not necessarily make her a progressive. Her views on race meant black suffragettes found themselves at odds with her views and were often excluded from the discussion entirely.

## A LASTING LEGACY

Though women did not win the right to vote during Anthony's lifetime, she never gave up her fight. Her persistence and hard work paid off when the 19th Amendment to the United States Constitution finally passed in 1919. It was ratified in 1920, officially providing the right for women to cast their ballots. Anthony's dedication and efforts are celebrated and honored each time a woman exercises her right to vote.

# CHANGE THE WORLD LIKE ANTHONY!

### ONE STEP AT A TIME

Anthony's efforts for women's suffrage unfolded over decades. She was in it for the long haul, methodically convincing people to join her cause. Have a big goal? Tackle it one step at a time— what is the very first action you need to take to get closer to success?

### BE INCLUSIVE

Anthony realized that women's opinions would be overlooked unless women had the right to vote. However, many proponents of women's suffrage overlooked the rights of women of color for decades (see page 118). When you are fighting to change the world for the better, take time to investigate how the issue at hand affects all kinds of people of different backgrounds and genders. Help make sure others' viewpoints and voices are heard as well.

PEOPLE DEMONSTRATING IN SUPPORT OF THE EQUAL RIGHTS AMENDMENT

## CHOOSING TRUTH

**SOJOURNER TRUTH** WAS AN ABOLITIONIST AND WOMEN'S RIGHTS ACTIVIST WHO IS MOST FAMOUS FOR HER IMPROVISED SPEECH "AIN'T I A WOMAN?"

Born as Isabella "Belle" Baumfree, Sojourner Truth (1797–November 26, 1883) spent the first 29 years of her life as a slave. She was bought and sold multiple times, endured violence, and had to fight to keep her children from being sold away from her. Her experiences would make her a vocal champion for the abolition, or end, of slavery. When Truth escaped to freedom with her daughter in 1826, she began speaking out against slavery and encouraged others to do the same. She had chosen her own destiny and also decided to choose her own name: Sojourner Truth. Truth felt called to spread truths about freedom and equality, thus beginning her career as a speaker and one of the most important activists in American history.

## AN IMPORTANT VOICE

Truth began to travel the country, speaking out against slavery and advocating for women's rights and prison reform. As her fame increased, she became interested in putting together her autobiography to further spread her message. But because Truth had been prevented from learning to read and write while she was enslaved, she could not write the book herself. Instead, she dictated it to a woman named Olive Gilbert, who then helped her publish the work. *Narrative of Sojourner Truth* gave a firsthand account of Truth's life and the evils of slavery. It also helped introduce Truth to women's rights activists Susan B. Anthony and Elizabeth Cady Stanton.

At the time, the women's suffrage movement was underway, but it did not represent all women. Truth quickly realized that the campaign for women's rights prioritized the perspectives of white women. Meanwhile, many antislavery advocates believed that women's rights should take a backseat to racial equality. Being both black and a woman, Truth brought a new and important view to many social movements.

## RIGHTS FOR ALL

Truth used her powerful voice to deliver one of the most important speeches in history in 1851 at the Ohio Women's Rights Convention. It came to be known as the "Ain't I a Woman?" speech and began when

**The man** over there says that women need to be helped into carriages and lifted over ditches, and to have the best place everywhere. Nobody ever helps me into carriages or over puddles or gives me the best place...

...and ain't I a woman? Look at my arm! I have ploughed and planted and gathered into barns, and no man could head me ...and ain't I a woman? I could work as much and eat as much as a man— when I could get it—and bear the lash as well ...and ain't I a woman? I have borne thirteen children, and seen most of 'em sold into slavery, and when I cried out with my mother's grief, none but Jesus heard me ...and ain't I a woman?

Sojourner Truth, Abolitionist, 1851

A POSTER WITH TRUTH'S PORTRAIT AND FAMOUS "AIN'T I A WOMAN?" SPEECH

# DEMAND

Truth stood up at the Women's Convention and requested a moment to speak. She emphasized both her womanhood and her race, two parts of her identity that were inseparable from each other. The only version of the speech known today was rewritten by Frances Dana Barker Gage, who is believed to have embellished the speech with dialect Truth may not have used. But Truth's message was clear: Some women whose experiences differed from those of leaders like Anthony and Stanton felt unseen by the larger women's suffrage movement. Truth called for the needs of black women, many of whom were still enslaved, to be included in conversations about women's rights.

Truth's speech was well received, and leaders within the women's rights movement left the meeting a bit wiser. More important, Truth's words would echo through history. Unfortunately, black women still face racially discriminatory voting laws and a lack of inclusivity in women's rights spaces. Though the work is far from over, Truth's legacy has empowered generations of black activists who continue to be inspired by her fight for inclusivity and equality.

Truth was one of the first black women to challenge a white man in a U.S. court— AND WIN!

# EQUALITY

# AMANI BALLOUR

The Syrian Civil War between ruling forces and rebels has been ongoing since 2011 and has resulted in enormous civilian casualties. In Ghouta, an area around the Syrian capital Damascus, pediatrician Dr. Amani Ballour has been fighting to save lives and bring national attention to the plight of Syria's people. Even amid the war, Dr. Ballour has managed to push back on societal expectations for women, becoming the first female doctor to manage a hospital in the area. Despite facing criticism for defying gender norms, Dr. Ballour continues to both save lives and use news and social media to call for action against the war.

## WHAT WOULD YOU SAY IS YOUR GREATEST STRENGTH?

 My greatest strength is my confidence in myself. I faced and overcame a lot of difficult things in the war and the siege in Syria—and in my society, which is controlled by men. I was the first woman to reach an important position of hospital leadership, at a very critical time. I support other women in their work, so we can all succeed.

## WHAT DO YOU THINK IS YOUR MOST CONSPICUOUS CHARACTER TRAIT?

 I'm very confident in what I do. I believe I can do the same job as a man can do; I don't think there is any difference. I trust myself.

## WHAT DO YOU THINK IS THE SINGLE MOST IMPORTANT CHANGE THAT NEEDS TO HAPPEN FOR WOMEN IN THE NEXT 10 YEARS?

 Despite all the progress made in the field of human rights, many women today still don't have the freedom to live as they want. Millions of women continue to live in inhumane conditions, deprived of their most basic rights. I would hope that someday any woman could get any education and take any job that she wanted.

## WHAT ADVICE WOULD YOU GIVE TO YOUNG WOMEN TODAY?

 I'd advise them to trust themselves and their personal abilities. To not give up their rights and goals under any circumstances, and to trust that their goals will be achieved one day.

# TARANA BURKE

Tarana Burke is a civil rights activist who focuses on gender and racial equality. In 2006, she began to use the phrase "Me Too" to recognize the prevalence of sexual assault. In 2017, #MeToo began to trend on social media and became a global movement against sexual harassment and sexual assault. Burke also founded a nonprofit for young women of color called Just Be and is the senior director of Girls for Gender Equity, a nonprofit that promotes gender equality.

## WHAT ADVICE WOULD YOU GIVE YOUNG WOMEN TODAY?

**BURKE:** I'd give the same advice that elders gave me when I was younger, which is: Slow down. Everything doesn't have to happen right now. And, particularly for young people nowadays, I'd say that things don't have to be public, and your work doesn't have to be widely accepted by people, in order to be valid. If you want to make a real difference, then just keep your head down and do your work.

## WHAT DO YOU THINK IS THE MOST IMPORTANT CHALLENGE FACING WOMEN TODAY?

**BURKE:** I don't know that there's just one challenge that's more important. I think if you ask different people, they would have different answers. But all of it involves the ways that women are affected economically, physically, and professionally.

## WHAT DO YOU THINK IS THE BIGGEST CHANGE THAT NEEDS TO HAPPEN FOR WOMEN IN THE NEXT 10 YEARS?

**BURKE:** It's so many things. If women got equal pay, that wouldn't stop violence against women. If we stopped violence, it doesn't mean women would get paid equally. We have to work on different fronts with the same level of passion and commitment and conviction. I wouldn't pick one particular area because then the other areas would suffer. We need to move the needle on all these areas of injustice that women deal with.

**MANUELA SÁENZ Y AIZPURU** WAS AN ACTIVIST AND REVOLUTIONARY WHO HELPED MULTIPLE LATIN AMERICAN COUNTRIES GAIN INDEPENDENCE.

Sáenz officially rose to the **RANK OF GENERAL** in Bolívar's army.

# FIGHT FOR INDEPEN

## BECOMING A REBEL

Manuela Sáenz y Aizpuru (December 27, 1797–November 23, 1856) was born in Quito, Ecuador, to a noble Spanish father and a poor Ecuadorian mother. Sáenz was raised by nuns at the Convent of Santa Catalina, where she learned to read and write. After leaving the convent, she married James Thorne, an English nobleman. They moved to Lima, Peru, where they hosted many parties attended by many important military leaders. But Sáenz was more than a hostess who enjoyed lavish gatherings.

At the time, the Spanish Empire (15th to 19th centuries) had controlled Peru for centuries, having invaded and destroyed the native Inca civilization in the 1500s. Many Peruvian citizens—including Sáenz—were tired of Spanish rule and longed for independence. She began secretly passing the military gossip she heard at parties to rebel forces across the country. But she wanted to do more, so Sáenz left her husband and returned to Quito, where she could take her involvement in the rebellion to the next level.

## THE REBELLION CONTINUES

Shortly after moving back to Quito, Sáenz met Simón Bolívar, a Venezuelan military leader. The pair fell in love, and Sáenz joined Bolívar's rebel army. She continued her spy work, gathering valuable information and keeping Bolívar's most important strategy documents, which put her at great risk. When Bolívar was nearly killed in an assassination attempt, Sáenz helped him escape. By saving him, she had protected the future freedom of Latin America, which earned her the nickname *libertadora del libertador*—"the liberator of the liberator."

## POWERFUL LEGACY

Peru officially won independence at the Battle of Ayacucho, a fight that Sáenz witnessed and that ensured freedom for the rest of Latin America. But after Bolívar's death in 1830, Sáenz was exiled from Colombia because her ties to the resistance made her an enemy to many political leaders. Sáenz ended up in a small town in Peru named Paita. She spent the rest of her life there until her death on November 23, 1856. Originally she was buried in a mass grave, but in 2010, symbolic remains from Sáenz's grave were transported through the countries she helped liberate and laid to rest in Venezuela next to Bolívar's remains. Sáenz's legacy as a fierce fighter for independence continues to inspire generations of people.

## CHANGE THE WORLD LIKE SÁENZ!

### EVERY ACTION COUNTS

Sáenz devoted her life to fighting for independence and was committed to actions small and large—from keeping track of important documents to saving lives. When you have a worthy goal, be willing to tackle both the big picture and the small details.

ART SHOWING THE PERUVIAN WAR OF INDEPENDENCE AGAINST THE SPANISH

# DENCE

HEATHER KOLDEWEY

IMOGEN NAPPER

EMILY DUNCAN

## AN OCEAN OF PLASTIC

Think about all the things you use every day that are made of plastic: bags, cups, containers, straws ... the list goes on and on. When you're finished using them, these items don't disappear. They have to go somewhere, and, unfortunately, approximately nine million tons (8 t) of plastic enter the ocean every single year. Worse, plastic never really goes away or biodegrades, and it negatively affects Earth's ecosystems. Marine life often mistakes plastic pollution, such as bags and straws, for food and eats it, or else gets caught in plastic containers and packaging. If things continue on the way they have been, the ocean could soon be destroyed beyond repair. But the female scientists of the National Geographic Society (NGS) Plastics Team are working hard to track plastic waste and prevent more of it from reaching the ocean.

## WOMEN LEADING THE WAY

The all-women NGS Plastics Team is made up of women from the United States and the United Kingdom who have expertise in multiple fields. Together they are documenting how plastic waste has affected the ocean, wildlife, and human communities. Meet the team:

### HEATHER KOLDEWEY

Koldewey is a conservation scientist and NGS Fellow whose work has taken her all over the world. She focuses on finding global conservation solutions that work for both people and the planet. Koldewey often provides crucial research on threatened species to government officials making policies that will impact the planet. Her work helped establish the Chagos Archipelago in the Indian Ocean as a marine reserve.

### JENNA JAMBECK

Jambeck is an environmental engineer and an expert on waste. She researches ways communities transport and dispose of solid waste such as plastics. To help find sustainable solutions to end marine pollution, she co-developed Marine Debris

# CLEAN UP THE PLANET

Tracker, an app that is designed to help everyday citizens track the garbage polluting the ocean. Through this app, more than one million pieces of marine debris have been removed from the environment.

LILLYGOL SEDAGHAT

others to be conscious of the way they consume products and materials. Sedaghat creatively uses visual art and digital media to help educate people about plastics and pollutions and to inspire the world to act.

## IMOGEN NAPPER

Napper is a marine scientist focused on the tiniest pieces of plastic in the ocean. Microplastic—pieces of plastic smaller than five millimeters—threatens marine life. Luckily, Napper is on the case. Her advocacy influenced banning microplastic beads from cosmetics on a global scale. She was also the first to conduct research about synthetic fibers in our clothing coming off during washing and contributing to waste in the ocean.

## LILLYGOL SEDAGHAT

Sedaghat is an environmental journalist who documents new and exciting ideas in waste management and recycling. Her goal is to inspire

## EMILY DUNCAN

Duncan is a marine researcher who earned her Ph.D. by investigating the impact of plastic pollution on sea turtle populations. She studied how plastics affect turtles' lives, from their diet to their nesting habits. Duncan is currently the head of an all-female crew of scientists and sailors who are sailing from the U.S. state of Hawaii to Vancouver, Canada, and collecting samples for research and to save sea turtles.

Each of these women is using her strengths and skills to tackle a global problem head-on. Through collaboration and innovation, the NGS Plastics Team is harnessing the power of science to improve the world!

# CHANGE THE WORLD LIKE THE NGS PLASTICS TEAM!

## CUT BACK ON PLASTIC

Reducing plastic use is critical to our planet's health. For tips on making your own reusable totes and lunch bags, hosting plastic-free parties, and more unique ways to cut down on plastic, grab a parent or guardian and visit Kids vs. Plastic on the National Geographic Kids site: *kids.nationalgeographic.com/explore/nature/kids-vs-plastic/* . You can also consider asking an adult to download Jambeck's Marine Debris Tracker to help reduce pollution.

## GET INVOLVED!

Ask an adult to help you find local cleanup projects or environmental groups that you can join. If there aren't any in your area, come up with your own plan to reduce waste in your community!

Jenna Jambeck is getting to the source of the PLASTIC PROBLEM.

JENNA JAMBECK

# INSPIRE CHANGE

**MARSHA P. JOHNSON** AND **SYLVIA RIVERA** WERE TRANSGENDER WOMEN DEVOTED TO LGBTQIA RIGHTS AND THE LGBTQIA CIVIL RIGHTS MOVEMENT.

The **FIRST GAY PRIDE MARCHES** occurred in 1970 in New York City, Los Angeles, and Chicago.

## SIMILAR STARTS

Marsha P. Johnson (August 24, 1945–July 6, 1992) and Sylvia Rivera (July 2, 1951–February 19, 2002) grew up in different cities, but both faced similarly difficult childhoods. Johnson was born as Malcolm Michaels, Jr., in Elizabeth, New Jersey, U.S.A., as one of seven children. She often wore dresses as a child but was harassed and forced to stop. Deeply unhappy, Johnson left home after high school and moved to New York City, where she was homeless. At the time, being gay, lesbian, transgender, or queer was unacceptable in much of America, and lesbian, gay, bisexual, transgender, queer or questioning, intersex, and asexual or allied (LGBTQIA) people even faced discriminatory laws in many states. Many young people were turned out of their homes, and a person known to be LGBTQIA faced heavy discrimination and difficulty just finding a job or housing. Luckily, Johnson found support in the local gay community. As she became more settled, she in turn began to help other homeless LGBTQIA youths—including Rivera.

Rivera had been born and raised in New York City. Born Ray Rivera to a Venezuelan mother and a Puerto Rican father, she was orphaned at just three years old and raised by her grandmother. But when she began wearing makeup, Rivera was deeply bullied both at school and home. She ran away at age 11 and lived on the city streets. Luckily, she met Johnson, and the two formed a close friendship.

## BREAKING POINT

Though Johnson and Rivera had found each other, they still faced incredible hardships. Police unfairly raided gay establishments and arrested gay and transgender people for no reason other than the fact that they were being themselves. On June 28, 1969, the police descended on the Stonewall Inn, a place known to be welcoming to some of society's most marginalized

RIVERA AND JOHNSON PICTURED AT LEFT ALONG WITH OTHER DEMONSTRATORS

people, including homeless youths, and gay, lesbian, and transgender people. But that night the patrons of the Stonewall Inn—including Rivera and Johnson—had had enough. They began a powerful protest against the police raid that gained national attention. As more and more demonstrators joined in night after night, the Stonewall uprising marked a turning point for gay rights.

After Stonewall, Johnson and Rivera continued fighting for their civil rights, joining the Gay Liberation Front and staging sit-in protests at New York University. Together, they also founded Street Transvestite Action Revolutionaries, an organization devoted to providing shelter and services for homeless transgender youths. Unfortunately, while the gay rights movement forged ahead, it excluded both people of color and transgender people. Johnson and Rivera still faced

discrimination, and, in 1973, they were even barred from joining New York City's gay pride parade. But the pair refused to sit on the sidelines and proudly marched to the front of the parade anyway.

## HONORING HER MEMORY

Johnson and Rivera continued their friendship and their defiant activism for many years, though, sadly, Johnson was found dead in 1992. Rivera continued their history-making fight for LGBTQIA rights and expanded her efforts to combat poverty. She remained devoted to her cause until her death in 2002. The Sylvia Rivera Law Project, founded in Rivera's honor, still provides education, legal services, and health care for queer and transgender people today. Both Johnson and Rivera are remembered as icons of inclusion and social change.

RIVERA (LEFT) AT A GAY LIBERATION DEMONSTRATION AT NEW YORK UNIVERSITY IN 1970

MARSHA P. JOHNSON

# ALICIA GARZA

Alicia Garza is an American civil rights activist who co-founded Black Lives Matter—a social movement that fights against systemic violence and racism toward black people—following the shooting of an unarmed black teen named Trayvon Martin. Garza posted a speech using the phrase "Black Lives Matter" to social media, and both it and the hashtag #BlackLivesMatter went viral. The now international organization also seeks to support black members of the LGBTQIA community and other marginalized groups.

## WHAT DO YOU THINK IS THE SINGLE MOST IMPORTANT CHANGE THAT NEEDS TO HAPPEN FOR WOMEN IN THE NEXT 10 YEARS?

 I think the most important thing is building power. Women need to be in positions to make decisions about our own lives and the lives of the people that we care about. As long as we're underrepresented in positions of power and the decision-making bodies, then it's going to be a big challenge to get the things that we need and want for our futures.

## WHAT IS YOUR GREATEST STRENGTH?

 My greatest strength is my ability to ignore when I get no for an answer. When people tell me it cannot be done, it must not be done, it has never been done, there's something that goes off inside of me that says, "Okay, watch me."

## WHAT ADVICE WOULD YOU GIVE TO YOUNG WOMEN TODAY?

 Keep going. There are so many things that tell us to stop doing what we're doing. Just keep going. Belong to yourself. Hold yourself to a high standard of integrity because that will take you farther than anything. Be bold. Take risks. Say sorry later.

# TARA HOUSKA

Tara Houska, Ojibwe from Couchiching First Nation, is a tribal attorney who specializes in legal advocacy for native peoples as well as environmental law. Houska spent six months in North Dakota opposing the Dakota Access Pipeline, an oil pipeline that poses environmental concerns to the Standing Rock Indian Reservation in North Dakota and South Dakota. She has since moved home to Minnesota to fight against Line 3, another pipeline that could cause harm to the Great Lakes ecosystem and tribal territories. Houska is also a co-founder of Not Your Mascots, a nonprofit organization dedicated to fighting stereotypes of indigenous peoples.

## WHAT IS YOUR GREATEST STRENGTH?

 Keeping my feet firmly on the ground.

## WHAT ADVICE WOULD YOU GIVE TO YOUNG WOMEN TODAY?

 Do not be afraid, stand strong. Feel the love of your ancestors behind you and the love of women from all walks of life who are cheering on your ferocity.

## WHAT DO YOU THINK IS THE SINGLE MOST IMPORTANT THING THAT NEEDS TO HAPPEN FOR WOMEN IN THE NEXT 10 YEARS?

 Women across the board must step into leadership roles. Politically, structurally, and within communities; the change is long overdue. My people's teachings prophesied a time when women would step into the forefront. That time is now.

## WHAT IS THE MOST IMPORTANT CHALLENGE FACING WOMEN TODAY?

 To love ourselves and one another. Women can overcome the many obstacles we face, but only if we hold each other up with clear hearts and minds.

# LEAD REBELLIONS

**TRUNG TRAC AND TRUNG NHI** WERE SISTERS WHO LED A VIETNAMESE REBELLION AGAINST THE CONQUERING ANCIENT CHINESE HAN DYNASTY.

## TWO SISTERS

In 111 B.C.E., the powerful Chinese Han dynasty (206 B.C.E.–220 C.E.) conquered the area of modern-day Vietnam, then known as the kingdom of Nam Viet. Around 100 years later, though their exact birthdates are unknown, sisters Trung Trac and Trung Nhi were born to a rural military family. Though Chinese women had few rights at the time, Vietnamese women had much more freedom and independence. The Trung sisters grew up studying the art of war, training in martial arts, and despising the brutal rule of the Han dynasty governors. Trung Trac met and married a like-minded man, Lord Thi Sach. Thi Sach also hated the oppressive regime and was unwilling to watch the Chinese tighten their grasp over Nam Viet. He organized other lords to take a stand, but the Chinese quickly assassinated him—and all the lords who stood with him. The brutal act made Trung Trac a widow.

## REVOLT

Though the Chinese intended for the deaths to be a warning message, Thi Sach's death had the opposite effect on the Trung sisters. In 39 C.E., they expelled Chinese troops from their village and rallied an army of supporters, made up largely of female soldiers. Including 8,000 soldiers and 36 female generals, one of whom was their mother, the sisters led a revolt. In just two months, the rebellion forces took back about 65 fortresses from the Chinese and liberated all of Nam Viet. Having led their kingdom to freedom, the sisters then proclaimed themselves queens. Though the Chinese launched several counterattacks, the Trung sisters and their army successfully held them off for more than two years.

Unwilling to give up Nam Viet, the Chinese had experienced general Ma Yuan amass a huge army and march against the Trung sisters in 43 C.E. Despite their valor, the

A PERSON WORSHIPPING AT A TEMPLE DEDICATED TO THE TRUNG SISTERS IN VIETNAM

It's believed that the Trung sisters rode into battle on the **BACKS OF ELEPHANTS.**

sisters and their soldiers were no match for the experienced Chinese troops. The Han army crushed the last of the Vietnam rebellion. Sources differ on what became of the sisters; some say they were defeated by Ma Yuan himself, and others claim that they jumped to their deaths in the Hát River rather than accept defeat.

## LEGACY

Though the Trung sisters' rebellion was defeated, the nation they fought for was not. They led the first Vietnamese resistance movement, and many more were to come. Today, the sisters remain revered symbols of Vietnamese independence, with many temples built in their honor and an annual February holiday to mark their deaths. Some historians believe that the Trung sisters' story offers evidence of a time when Vietnam was a matriarchal society, encouraging women to lead and rule. To this day, they are icons for female leaders, soldiers, and revolutionaries.

# CHANGE THE WORLD LIKE THE TRUNG SISTERS!

### BE YOUR OWN HERO

The Trung sisters knew they couldn't wait for someone else to organize a rebellion, so they did it themselves. When something in the world needs improvement, instead of waiting for another person to step up, consider whether that person might be you.

### TAKE A STAND

The Trung sisters chose to defend their country—as well as their independence and freedom—rather than watch them be taken away. Know your rights and stand up for them when they're at risk.

A LOOK INSIDE A TEMPLE DEDICATED TO THE TRUNG SISTERS IN THEIR BIRTHPLACE OF NORTHWEST HANOI, VIETNAM

# PROTECT THE ENVIRONMENT

**ADJANY COSTA** IS A BIOLOGIST, CONSERVATIONIST, AND NATIONAL GEOGRAPHIC EXPLORER WHO WORKS TO PROTECT WILDLIFE AND THEIR HABITATS.

Costa ate almost nothing but **RICE AND BEANS** while she was on the Okavango Delta expedition.

## ENVIRONMENTAL EXPERT

Born in Angola on August 12, 1989, Adjany Costa's first memories were of the civil war that tore through her country. But Costa also had happy memories: Every year, her family visited the beach, where she fell in love with the water. It wasn't until Costa first saw the movie *The Little Mermaid*, though, that she realized she wanted to spend her life in the water among the fish! Biology and conservation were not common fields in Angola at the time, but Costa's parents encouraged her to follow her dreams. Soon, others began to take notice of Costa's skills and passion, including National Geographic Fellow Steve Boyes. He was launching an expedition to explore Africa's Okavango Delta and invited Costa to join. It wouldn't be easy—the project would last for four months as they explored 1,500 miles (2,414 km) of wilderness, facing dangerous wild animals and the elements. Costa said yes.

## EXPLORING THE OKAVANGO DELTA

In May 2015, Costa set out with a group of scientists and explorers on the first expedition of the National Geographic Okavango Wilderness Project. Their mission was to navigate, study, and protect one of the largest freshwater wetlands in southern Africa: the Okavango Delta. The delta, which starts as a series of rivers in Angola, is a large wetland that is formed as the rivers disperse into the sands. It supports a huge amount of biodiversity and is also a water source for one million people. Unfortunately, the Okavango Delta is at risk of disappearing, due to hunting, land clearing for farming, and a lack of protection.

As the assistant director of the expedition and expert on marine biology, Costa helped record the types of marine life they saw. She encountered charging elephants and hippos, was bitten by spiders and scorpions, and stung by countless bees. But she persevered and has contributed vital information to conservation efforts. These days, Costa continues to focus on preserving the Okavango Delta and plans to expand her efforts to establish a protected marine area off of Angola. She hopes that her work brings new opportunities and hope to the people of Angola, and to the entire planet.

# SAVE ANIMALS

## THE EFFECTS OF WAR

Dominique Gonçalves was born in 1992, the same year that the Mozambican Civil War (1977–1992) ended. Unfortunately, the war had done unthinkable damage; homes and lands were destroyed, and more than one million people were killed. The country's animals had suffered too—in the Gorongosa National Park (GNP), more than 95 percent of the large animals died. Gonçalves grew up seeing the suffering first-hand—and she wanted to do something about it.

## BRINGING COMMUNITY TOGETHER

Though she endured extreme poverty—including hunger and a lack of shoes and clothes—while pursuing her studies, Gonçalves earned her degree in conservation biology. Soon after, she joined the GNP as the manager of the Elephant Ecology Project, where she studied elephant movement and habits, as well as ways to reduce human-elephant conflict. Her work has helped to make an enormous impact on elephant conservation within the park. After the war, the elephant population numbered less than 200—down from more than 2,000 elephants in 1969. But thanks to conservation efforts by Gonçalves and others, the park had more than 800 elephants at the end of 2017, and their numbers are still increasing. The same is true for animal species across the park—though only 10,000 large animals survived at the end of the war, they now number more than 80,000.

In addition to aiding animals and their habitats, Gonçalves and the other members of the GNP work equally hard to support the local communities. Their goal is to encourage surrounding communities to protect the park and also to benefit from it. Gonçalves and the GNP have established health care programs, promoted education for girls, and created job opportunities. The park employs more than 500 people, 98 percent of whom are Mozambican—including the park's first ever female rangers. By working to help both her country and its animals, Gonçalves has created a bridge between the wildlife within the park and the people who live near it. Today, Gonçalves aims to train new generations of conservationists and researchers and create a brighter future for the world.

**DOMINIQUE GONÇALVES** IS AN ECOLOGIST AND NATIONAL GEOGRAPHIC FELLOW DEDICATED TO ELEPHANT CONSERVATION.

Gonçalves works closely with the GNP's girls' club programs to **PROMOTE GIRLS' EDUCATION.**

133

# BOYS CAN, TOO!

HAVE YOU EVER HEARD THAT **BOYS SHOULDN'T CRY?**

For women to change the world, they have had to smash tons of stereotypes and destroy gender biases. As it turns out, although stereotypes do directly and indirectly prevent girls from reaching their full potential, they are harmful to everyone. Boys and men who show interest in things that aren't "manly" enough often face bullying. Studies found that the pressure to conform to traditional gender roles can create health risks in children as young as 10 and negatively impact boys' learning, motivation, and feelings of self-worth. Fortunately, people are fighting these stereotypes and busting myths that boys can't do something just because they're boys. Here are a few of the things boys can do, even when they're told they can't!

### BOYS CAN'T CRY

Boys are often told to "stop crying" and encouraged to hide their emotions. Many people view crying as weak or feminine and pressure boys to bottle up their feelings from a young age. But studies show that crying and expressing emotions is natural for all genders. Scientists say that young girls and boys naturally cry an equal amount and that there are no neurological differences in men's or women's abilities to feel. In fact, in a study of more than 500,000 people, men rated just as high as women in emotional awareness. Plus, boys who are encouraged to express their emotions tend to do better in school and are also emotionally healthier later in life.

## BOYS CAN'T BE CARING

Boys are often expected to follow traditional career paths and to be the primary earners for their families. But just as women are equally capable in the professional world, men are as good as women at cleaning, cooking, raising children, and taking on caretaker roles. In the United States, men often feel discouraged from pursuing traditionally nurturing jobs. Only 9 percent of U.S. nurses are male, and only 23 percent of teachers are male, and the numbers for men of color are even smaller. But studies show that men excel in these areas. They should be encouraged to follow their passions—whether that's nursing, teaching, or being a stay-at-home dad.

## BOYS CAN'T LIKE PINK

For the past century or so, much of society has believed that boys should not like "girly" things like makeup, dresses, or the color pink. As it turns out, this is totally bogus—and history can prove it. Though many people may believe that pink is for girls, pink was actually considered a masculine color from the 18th century through the early 1900s. Because it is a similar shade to red, many people thought of it as "warlike" and associated it with boys.

And it wasn't until the past century or so that it was considered unusual for men to wear makeup. Men regularly painted their faces from 4000 B.C.E., when the ancient Egyptians were rocking kohl eyeliner, all the way up to the 1700s, when men in Europe were powdering their faces, wearing wigs, and even drawing on beauty marks. It turns out that men have been wearing makeup for more of history than not!

Pants are also a relatively new invention. In ancient societies like those of the Greeks, Romans, and Egyptians, men wore robes and tunics, and many cultures around the world still consider those garments masculine. It wasn't until the European Renaissance between the 14th and 17th centuries that pants—then pantaloons—became the norm. Today, tons of male makeup beauty gurus and fashionistas are disregarding traditional norms and are dazzling in all kinds of outfits.

## CHANGE THE WORLD!

You probably already know that it's not easy to overcome stereotypes. So if you get the chance to support another person following their own path, take it. Stand up for people who express themselves differently, and make sure you are welcoming to newcomers who want to try out activities, styles, or hobbies that they might not usually join.

# QUESTIONS FOR DISCUSSION

**ACROSS THE GLOBE, WOMEN HAVE MADE MAJOR CONTRIBUTIONS TO ART, SCIENCE, MEDICINE, LITERATURE, AND POLITICS. In modern times, women have invented amazing things, such as Kevlar (Stephanie Kwolek) and ice-cream makers (Nancy Johnson). Why are female leaders (warriors, scientists, explorers ...) still considered the exception, not the rule? What are the social and political consequences of full equality of the sexes?**

▶▶ History reflects who gets to write it. Have you heard of Elizabeth Friedman? She was a pioneer of cryptography whose work laid the foundation for today's American intelligence service. She isn't a household name because powerful men not only took credit for her work but also erased her name from official records. Her example is not unique. If other women have been written out of history, how do you go about finding them? What does it mean to write "herstories" instead of "histories"?

**Suggested reading:**

- Blair Imani, *Modern HERstory: Stories of Women and Nonbinary People Rewriting History*

- Liza Mundy, *Code Girls: The Untold Story of the American Women Code Breakers of World War II,* Young Readers Edition

▶▶ Imagine you are a journalist. Are women in your community (such as your mom, an aunt, a sister) doing incredible things that only you know about? What if the stories you want to tell are dangerous? In the late 19th and early 20th centuries, for example, a black reporter named Ida B. Wells investigated lynching, the violent mob executions by hanging, specifically targeted at black people. Her columns so enraged locals that she was forced to flee to save her own life. Do you think that women should not practice investigative journalism because of the dangers they face? Is it important to reveal the truth, no matter the cost?

**Suggested reading:**

- Deborah Noyes, *Ten Days a Madwoman: The Daring Life and Turbulent Times of the Original "Girl" Reporter, Nellie Bly*

- Roxanne Dunbar-Ortiz, adapted by Jean Mendoza and Debbie Reese, *An Indigenous Peoples' History of the United States for Young People*

▶▶ "You fight like a girl" is supposed to be an insult. In the American Civil War, however, women disguised themselves as men and fought on the front lines. In other wars, women contributed by becoming codebreakers, assassins, and spies. Today, military forces include female combatants, and an armed, all-female group called the Black Mambas fights poaching in Africa. Why does the stereotype persist that women are not brave enough to fight, whether it be fighting in war or fighting against injustice more generally?

**Suggested reading:**

- Russell Freedman, *We Will Not Be Silent: The White Rose Student Resistance Movement That Defied Adolf Hitler*

- Ann McCallum Staats, *Women Heroes of the US Army: Remarkable Soldiers From the American Revolution to Today*

▶▶ The anonymous author of *Frankenstein* was a teen named Mary Shelley. The Bell brothers were actually the Brontë sisters. Robert Galbraith is the pen name of Joanne Rowling, better known as J. K. Rowling, author of the Harry Potter series. Can you think of other situation in which girls and women might hide their gender by assuming a male persona in public? What are the pros and cons of doing this?

**Suggested reading:**

- Chris Barton, *Can I See Your I.D.?: True Stories of False Identities*

▶▶ It used to be considered the height of masculinity to curl your long hair, wear silk tights, and show off your toned calves in fashionable high heels. (Just look at some royal portraits prior to the 19th century.) Today, we think that only girls and women are supposed to wear these items. If you were alone on a deserted island where nobody would judge you for your appearance, how do you think you'd dress? How is clothing and makeup used to express—and repress—personal identities?

**Suggested reading:**

- Sarah Albee, *Why'd They Wear That?*

▶▶ "A woman's place is in the home." Who first said this and why? Have you ever been told that you can't be a _____ simply because you're a girl? Come up with some alternative endings to the phrase: "A woman's place is in _____," and then put on your historian's hat and find examples of women who have accomplished that goal.

**Suggested reading:**

- Olugbemisola Rhuday-Perkovich, *Above and Beyond: NASA's Journey to Tomorrow*

- Penny Colman, *Rosie the Riveter: Women Working on the Home Front in World War II*

▶▶ Women who challenged social norms used to be denounced as witches. Today, women who don't fit neatly into predetermined boxes are still often treated as dangers to the social order. Why do humans so often fear the exceptional and extraordinary? What are some inventive ways to expand social expectations of how girls should behave and be?

**Suggested reading:**

- Marvel Hero Project graphic novels

- Rosalyn Schanzer, *Witches! The Absolutely True Tale of Disaster in Salem*

▶▶ As you have learned from this book, it used to be illegal for women to work, to hold property, to vote, and so on. Who wrote these laws? Who upholds them? How are laws made—and how are they changed? In 1911, for example, a disastrous fire in the Triangle Shirtwaist Factory, which primarily employed women, led to a groundbreaking fight for the rights of all American workers. Similarly, the fight for Title IX reveals how federal laws impact the right of girls to compete in sports. Can you find other laws that you think are unjust? How would you go about changing them?

**Suggested reading:**

- Albert Marrin, *Flesh and Blood So Cheap: The Triangle Fire and Its Legacy*

- Emma Gray, *A Girl's Guide to Joining the Resistance: A Feminist Handbook on Fighting for Good*

# INDEX

Boldface indicates illustrations.

# INDEX

# CREDITS

Since 1888, the National Geographic Society has funded more than 12,000 research, exploration, and preservation projects around the world. The Society receives funds from National Geographic Partners, LLC, funded in part by your purchase. A portion of the proceeds from this book supports this vital work. To learn more, visit natgeo.com/info.

NATIONAL GEOGRAPHIC and Yellow Border Design are trademarks of the National Geographic Society, used under license.

For more information, visit nationalgeographic.com, call 1-877-873-6846, or write to the following address:

National Geographic Partners
1145 17th Street N.W.
Washington, D.C. 20036-4688 U.S.A.

Visit us online at nationalgeographic.com/books

For librarians and teachers: nationalgeographic.com
/books/librarians-and-educators

More for kids from National Geographic:
natgeokids.com

*National Geographic Kids* magazine inspires children to explore their world with fun yet educational articles on animals, science, nature, and more. Using fresh storytelling and amazing photography, *Nat Geo Kids* shows kids ages 6 to 14 the fascinating truth about the world—and why they should care.
**kids.nationalgeographic.com/subscribe**

For rights or permissions inquiries, please contact National Geographic Books Subsidiary Rights:
bookrights@natgeo.com

Designed by Amanda Larsen and Shannon Pallatta

Trade Hardcover ISBN: 978-1-4263-3900-4
Reinforced library binding ISBN: 978-1-4263-3901-1

The publisher would like to thank everyone who helped make this book possible:
Ariane Szu-Tu, editor; Catherine Frank, text editor; Rebecca Baines, editorial director;
Lori Epstein, photo director; Molly Reid, production editor; Jennifer Geddes, fact-checker;
Trudy Hong and Corinne Mercedes, legal counsel; and Paula Lee and author Dr. Ilene Wong
for their sensitivity reviews.

Printed in Hong Kong
20/PPHK/1

A SPECIAL THANKS TO LILY, ALEXA, AND TEAGAN, OUR CAN-DO COVER SHOOT LADIES!